THIS BOOK BELONGS TO

_____

START DATE

_____

SHE READS TRUTH

EXECUTIVE

FOUNDER/CHIEF EXECUTIVE OFFICER
Raechel Myers

CO-FOUNDER/CHIEF CONTENT OFFICER
Amanda Bible Williams

CHIEF OPERATING OFFICER
Ryan Myers

EDITORIAL

CONTENT DIRECTOR
Jessica Lamb

DIGITAL MANAGING EDITOR
Oghosa Iyamu, MDiv

PRODUCTION EDITOR
Hannah Little, MTS

MARKETING CONTENT EDITOR
Tameshia Williams, ThM

ASSOCIATE EDITORS
Kayla De La Torre, MAT
Lindsey Jacobi, MDiv

COPY EDITOR
Becca Owens, MA

MARKETING

MARKETING DIRECTOR
Kamron Kunce

GROWTH MARKETING MANAGER
Blake Showalter

PRODUCT MARKETING MANAGER
Megan Phillips

SOCIAL MEDIA STRATEGIST
Taylor Krupp

CREATIVE

CREATIVE DIRECTOR
Amy Dennis

DESIGN MANAGER
Kelsea Allen

DESIGNERS
Abbey Benson
Amanda Brush, MA
Annie Glover
Lauren Haag

JUNIOR DESIGNER
Jessie Gerakinis

OPERATIONS

OPERATIONS DIRECTOR
Allison Sutton

OFFICE MANAGER
Nicole Quirion

PROJECT ASSISTANT
Mary Beth Montgomery

SHIPPING

SHIPPING MANAGER
Marian Byne

FULFILLMENT LEAD
Cait Baggerman

FULFILLMENT SPECIALIST
Kajsa Matheny

SUBSCRIPTION INQUIRIES
orders@shereadstruth.com

COMMUNITY SUPPORT

COMMUNITY EXPERIENCE DIRECTOR
Kara Hewett, MOL

COMMUNITY SUPPORT SPECIALISTS
Katy McKnight
Alecia Rohrer
Heather Vollono

@SHEREADSTRUTH

Download the She Reads Truth app,
available for iOS and Android

Subscribe to the
She Reads Truth podcast

SHEREADSTRUTH.COM

This book was printed offset in Nashville, Tennessee, on 70# Lynx Opaque. Cover is 100# Cougar Opaque with a soft touch lamination.

THE GENEALOGY OF JESUS

GOD'S LOYALTY FROM GENERATION TO GENERATION

RESTORATION IS
HIS SPECIALTY.

Raechel Myers
**FOUNDER/CHIEF
EXECUTIVE OFFICER**

Family is messy.

Were I to roll out a huge expanse of paper and sketch out my family tree with honest stories and details in black and white, complicated wouldn't begin to describe it. Our branches are broken and split and mended and a little twisty. The fruit is abundant in some places and absent in others, sour and sweet and rotten and ripe.

But if I switched pens to another color (let's say red for the obvious symbolic win of it), and overlaid notes of unexplainable restoration, against-all-odds redemption, and threads of hope binding us up and not letting us go...well, that would be a story we couldn't write on our own if we tried. And all with that same cast of characters—sour and sweet and rotten and ripe though we may be.

My parents divorced when I was seven and my nuclear family shape and headcount changed at least once a year after that until I was a teenager. I couldn't have guessed it then, but the very weekend my parents separated, we went to a new church and I met the boy who would one day grow up to be the kind husband and invested father I missed out on in my childhood. (Yes, I remember meeting him! And no, I'll never get over the specifically noteworthy kindness of God at work in my seven-year-old life.)

What I've learned is that to label any person in our stories as a hero or a villain is incomplete. No one is all good or all bad, as much as we'd sometimes prefer that distillation. But God is always good. Always. And as we like to say in our family, "Restoration is His specialty."

Need proof? This book contains five weeks of curated Scripture reading offering an up-close look at Jesus's biological family tree and at the spiritual family He brings us into. The men and women God wove into the lineage of the Redeemer include murderers, cheaters, abusers, repenters, forgivers, hopers, and believers. No villains, no heroes. Just a whole lot of people, like you and me, in need of the hope of the world.

Before you begin reading, take a look at the "Start Here" extra on page 14 for a broad view of Jesus's genealogies as well as a road map for the reading plan. As you read, spend time engaging with the daily response, reflecting on the themes and through lines of each story. My prayer is that you will be moved by the real human stories and the reality that, even in our own broken lives and families, God is still writing a far greater story.

Family is messy. And restoration is His specialty.

DESIGN ON PURPOSE

AT SHE READS TRUTH, WE BELIEVE IN PAIRING THE INHERENTLY BEAUTIFUL WORD OF GOD WITH THE AESTHETIC BEAUTY IT DESERVES. EACH OF OUR RESOURCES IS THOUGHTFULLY AND ARTFULLY DESIGNED TO HIGHLIGHT THE BEAUTY, GOODNESS, AND TRUTH OF SCRIPTURE IN A WAY THAT REFLECTS THE THEMES OF EACH CURATED READING PLAN.

Custom watercolor pieces are the centerpiece of this Study Book design. The movement of the watercolor contains places of deep pigment saturation, pointing to the heavier elements of grief, sin, and brokenness, as well as lighter saturation that reminds us of the more joyful experiences. These variations layer on top of one another to remind us of God's faithfulness to work through the broken, difficult, and beautiful aspects of human life from generation to generation.

We chose to layer a checkerboard pattern over other elements in this book. These smaller pieces point to the individual stories that make up the entire picture of God's spiritual family.

Botanical photographs featured throughout represent the hope of growth and flourishing even in seasons of barrenness. Both blurry and clear photos remind us of the imperfection and beauty that each of our own stories contain in Christ.

The time-worn serif font is paired with handwritten elements from different members of our team to represent the generations present in the genealogy of Jesus. These details anchor us in the humanity of this historic through line.

Then God said, "Let us make man in our image, according to our likeness. They will rule the fish of the sea, the birds of the sky, the livestock, the whole earth, and the creatures that crawl on the earth."

Genesis 1:26

HOW TO USE THIS BOOK

She Reads Truth is a community of women dedicated to reading the
Word of God every day. In **The Genealogy of Jesus** reading plan,
we will trace God's promise of abundant life, blessing, and flourishing
through the complexity of the human experience. We will see Jesus as
the redemptive culmination of a complicated family story, and see how
we as believers are participants in His family inheritance.

READ & REFLECT

Your **The Genealogy of Jesus**
Study Book focuses primarily on
Scripture, with added features
to come alongside your time
with God's Word.

SCRIPTURE READING

Designed for a Monday start, this
Study Book presents daily readings
that explore the spiritual and
physical family of Jesus.

*To aid in your reading experience,
Scripture passages are labeled with
each book's name headline and the
chapter subheading.*

REFLECTION QUESTIONS

Each weekday features questions
and space for personal response,
along with an extended moment
of reflection.

COMMUNITY & CONVERSATION

You can start reading this book at any time! If
you want to join women from Topeka to Taiwan
as they read along with you, the She Reads Truth
community will start Day 1 of **The Genealogy of
Jesus** on Monday, June 5, 2023.

 SHE READS TRUTH APP

For added community and conversation, join us in
The Genealogy of Jesus reading plan on the She
Reads Truth app. You can use the app to participate
in community discussion and more.

GRACE DAY

Use Saturdays to catch up on your reading, pray, and rest in the presence of the Lord.

WEEKLY TRUTH

Sundays are set aside for Scripture memorization.

See tips for memorizing Scripture on page 172.

EXTRAS

This book features additional tools to help you gain a deeper understanding of the text.

Find a complete list of extras on page 13.

 SHEREADSTRUTH.COM

The Genealogy of Jesus reading plan will also be available at SheReadsTruth.com as the community reads each day. Invite your family, friends, and neighbors to read along with you!

 SHE READS TRUTH PODCAST

Subscribe to the She Reads Truth podcast and join our founders and their guests each week as they talk about what you'll read in the week ahead.

 Podcast episodes 180–184 for our **The Genealogy of Jesus** *series release on Mondays beginning June 5, 2023.*

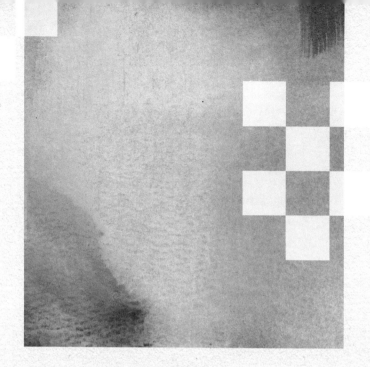

TABLE OF
CONTENTS

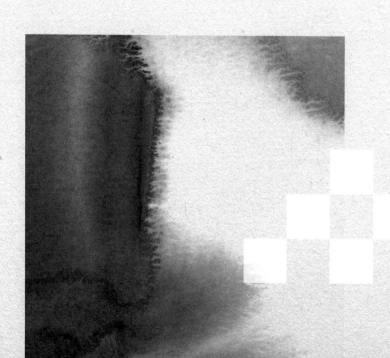

Start Here

The genealogy of Jesus points us to the greater story being woven throughout history. Understanding the framework of this reading plan will equip you for the weeks ahead. So before you jump into your daily Scripture reading, start here with an introduction to the bigger picture.

1/3

THE GENEALOGY OF JESUS

Two New Testament books, Matthew and Luke, include Jesus's family history in the form of a genealogy. These long accounts trace Jesus's ancestry from Abraham (in Matthew) and back to Adam (in Luke).

More than a list of names, these genealogies show God's faithfulness to work through the broken, difficult, and beautiful aspects of human life from generation to generation. His grand redemptive story happens through estranged families, heartbreak, betrayal, difficult moves, affairs, scandal, and infertility. It continues through the branches of deep friendship, marriages, beloved children, reconciliation, and adoption. God remains loyal to His promise, His purpose, and His people through every beautiful and painful reality.

BRANCHES AND ROOTS

This is a story of physical branches on a family tree. These relationships led to real sons, daughters, and heirs, culminating in the birth of a Jewish baby boy in the first century.

It is also a story of roots. Connected deeper than DNA or adoption into one family, God is at work beyond what is visible to bring people from all places to share in His promises. As believers, we are brought into this spiritual family through Jesus. In Him, we share in the spiritual and physical promises of the family of God.

IN THIS READING PLAN

01

The first day introduces God's promise to restore all things through a chosen people as His family. The second day looks at the two genealogies of Jesus, who fulfilled this promise.

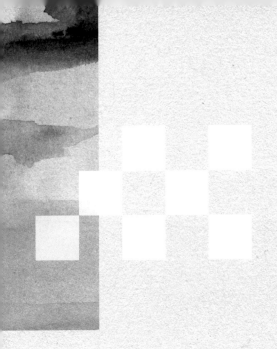

02

The rest of Week 1 covers the early stories of Jesus's family line, including how God created humans as image-bearers. He gave humans a unique role of stewardship, sharing in the responsibility of caring for all of God's creation. We'll see how sin marred our ability to reflect this image and carry out this purpose effectively. We will read how this blessing and invitation were distorted by sin, but were never lost. During this first week, you'll have unique questions to answer every day to set up your reading journey.

03

The last four weeks cover the stories of real people in the lineage of Jesus.

The reading plan concludes with Scripture on the gospel reality that believers are forever part of this family of God.

GENEALOGIES IN THE BIBLE

KEEP IN MIND...

01

Ancient genealogies were not meant as pure historical record. Instead, they were assembled to emphasize identity and status, legitimizing a person's rightful claim to a role (such as priest or king) or an inheritance.

02

Ancient genealogies could be linear, recording one individual for each generation, or segmented, dividing names into groups across the generations recorded.

03

Segmented genealogies were not comprehensive. Often, only a select number of representative generations and people were listed. (Fun tidbit: the scholarly term for this is telescoping.)

04

The genealogies emphasized family relationships, connecting key people in a person's history with one another. Fathered, son of, begat, and other words that we tend to read literally were used originally as broader terms to represent a line of descendants. For example, Rahab may have been Boaz's mother, but she also may have been his grandmother, or great-grandmother, or an ancestress even further back.

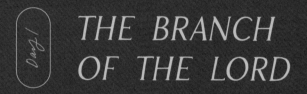

THE BRANCH OF THE LORD

The root running through the Old Testament is one of God making, calling, redeeming, and keeping a people for Himself—a physical people called to be a blessing to the world. This family tree would bring about the Branch that would be the world's salvation: Jesus who grafted us into a spiritual family.

EXODUS

FROM CHAPTER 4

²² "And you will say to Pharaoh: This is what the LORD says: Israel is my firstborn son."

DEUTERONOMY

FROM CHAPTER 7

⁷ The LORD had his heart set on you and chose you, not because you were more numerous than all peoples, for you were the fewest of all peoples. ⁸ But because the LORD loved you and kept the oath he swore to your ancestors, he brought you out with a strong hand and redeemed you from the place of slavery, from the power of Pharaoh king of Egypt. ⁹ Know that the LORD your God is God, the faithful God who keeps his gracious covenant loyalty for a thousand generations with those who love him and keep his commands.

JEREMIAH

FROM CHAPTER 23

³ "I will gather the remnant of my flock from all the lands where I have banished them, and I will return them to their grazing land. They will become fruitful and numerous. ⁴ I will raise up shepherds over them who will tend them. They will no longer be afraid or discouraged, nor will any be missing." This is the LORD's declaration.

Keep an eye out for margin notes on cultural elements in the genealogies as you read.

WHAT IS THE SIGNIFICANCE OF "FIRSTBORN SON"?

In the ancient world, inheritance and property passed down from father to son, with the firstborn son usually receiving priority. Daughters often had limited or restricted rights of inheritance, or sometimes none at all.

The Righteous Branch of David

⁵ "Look, the days are coming"—this is the
    Lᴏʀᴅ's declaration—
"when I will raise up a Righteous Branch for David.
He will reign wisely as king
and administer justice and righteousness in the land."

ISAIAH

FROM CHAPTER 4

Zion's Future Glory

² On that day the Branch of the Lᴏʀᴅ will be beautiful and
glorious, and the fruit of the land will be the pride and glory
of Israel's survivors.

FROM CHAPTER 11

Reign of the Davidic King

¹ Then a shoot will grow from the stump
    of Jesse,
and a branch from his roots will bear fruit.

² The Spirit of the Lᴏʀᴅ will rest on him—
a Spirit of wisdom and understanding,
a Spirit of counsel and strength,
a Spirit of knowledge and of the fear of the Lᴏʀᴅ.

…

Israel Regathered

¹⁰ On that day the root of Jesse
will stand as a banner for the peoples.
The nations will look to him for guidance,
and his resting place will be glorious.

FROM CHAPTER 53

¹ Who has believed what we have heard?
And to whom has the arm of the Lᴏʀᴅ been revealed?
² He grew up before him like a young plant
and like a root out of dry ground.
He didn't have an impressive form
or majesty that we should look at him,
no appearance that we should desire him.
³ He was despised and rejected by men,
a man of suffering who knew what sickness was.
He was like someone people turned away from;
he was despised, and we didn't value him.

⁴ Yet he himself bore our sicknesses,
and he carried our pains;
but we in turn regarded him stricken,
struck down by God, and afflicted.
⁵ But he was pierced because of our rebellion,
crushed because of our iniquities;
punishment for our peace was on him,
and we are healed by his wounds.

RESPONSE

Each of today's passages includes a visual picture or description of God's relationship to His people. Which one(s) do you notice? Write them below.

Exodus 4

Deuteronomy 7

Jeremiah 23

Isaiah 4

Isaiah 11

Isaiah 53

THE GENEALOGY OF JESUS

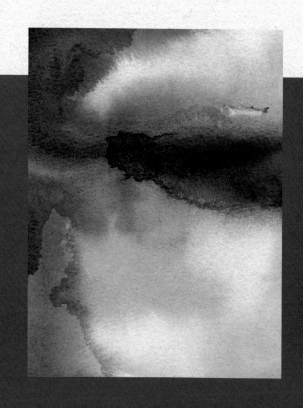

Day 2

MATTHEW

FROM CHAPTER 1

The Genealogy of Jesus Christ

[1] An account of the genealogy of Jesus Christ, the Son of David, the Son of Abraham:

From Abraham to David

[2] Abraham fathered Isaac,
Isaac fathered Jacob,
Jacob fathered Judah and his brothers,
[3] Judah fathered Perez and Zerah by Tamar,
Perez fathered Hezron,
Hezron fathered Aram,
[4] Aram fathered Amminadab,
Amminadab fathered Nahshon,
Nahshon fathered Salmon,
[5] Salmon fathered Boaz by Rahab,
Boaz fathered Obed by Ruth,
Obed fathered Jesse,
[6] and Jesse fathered King David.

From David to the Babylonian Exile

David fathered Solomon by Uriah's wife,
[7] Solomon fathered Rehoboam,
Rehoboam fathered Abijah,
Abijah fathered Asa,
[8] Asa fathered Jehoshaphat,
Jehoshaphat fathered Joram,
Joram fathered Uzziah,
[9] Uzziah fathered Jotham,
Jotham fathered Ahaz,
Ahaz fathered Hezekiah,
[10] Hezekiah fathered Manasseh,

WHY ARE THERE TWO DIFFERENT GENEALOGIES?

Matthew's genealogy traces Jesus's lineage from Abraham to Jesus. Writing primarily to a Jewish audience, Matthew used his genealogy to present Jesus as the fulfillment of long-anticipated Old Testament prophecies, including the covenant family of Abraham and the royal line of King David. Luke's genealogy begins with Jesus and traces His lineage all the way back to Adam. Luke used his genealogy to show Jesus's connection to the entirety of humanity. Though the two versions align at several points, scholars disagree about how to reconcile the perceived differences in each.

SHE READS TRUTH

DAY 2   25

Manasseh fathered Amon,
Amon fathered Josiah,
[11] and Josiah fathered Jeconiah and his brothers
at the time of the exile to Babylon.

From the Exile to the Messiah

[12] After the exile to Babylon
Jeconiah fathered Shealtiel,
Shealtiel fathered Zerubbabel,
[13] Zerubbabel fathered Abiud,
Abiud fathered Eliakim,
Eliakim fathered Azor,
[14] Azor fathered Zadok,
Zadok fathered Achim,
Achim fathered Eliud,
[15] Eliud fathered Eleazar,
Eleazar fathered Matthan,
Matthan fathered Jacob,
[16] and Jacob fathered Joseph the husband of Mary,
who gave birth to Jesus who is called the Messiah.

[17] So all the generations from Abraham to David were fourteen generations; and from David until the exile to Babylon, fourteen generations; and from the exile to Babylon until the Messiah, fourteen generations.

LUKE

FROM CHAPTER 3

The Genealogy of Jesus Christ

[23] As he began his ministry, Jesus was about thirty years old and was thought to be the

son of Joseph, son of Heli,
[24] son of Matthat, son of Levi,

son of Melchi, son of Jannai,
son of Joseph, [25] son of Mattathias,
son of Amos, son of Nahum,
son of Esli, son of Naggai,
[26] son of Maath, son of Mattathias,
son of Semein, son of Josech,
son of Joda, [27] son of Joanan,
son of Rhesa, son of Zerubbabel,
son of Shealtiel, son of Neri,
[28] son of Melchi, son of Addi,
son of Cosam, son of Elmadam,
son of Er, [29] son of Joshua,
son of Eliezer, son of Jorim,
son of Matthat, son of Levi,
[30] son of Simeon, son of Judah,
son of Joseph, son of Jonam,
son of Eliakim, [31] son of Melea,
son of Menna, son of Mattatha,
son of Nathan, son of David,
[32] son of Jesse, son of Obed,
son of Boaz, son of Salmon,
son of Nahshon, [33] son of Amminadab,
son of Ram, son of Hezron,
son of Perez, son of Judah,
[34] son of Jacob, son of Isaac,
son of Abraham, son of Terah,
son of Nahor, [35] son of Serug,
son of Reu, son of Peleg,
son of Eber, son of Shelah,
[36] son of Cainan, son of Arphaxad,
son of Shem, son of Noah,
son of Lamech, [37] son of Methuselah,
son of Enoch, son of Jared,
son of Mahalalel, son of Cainan,
[38] son of Enos, son of Seth,
son of Adam, son of God.

RESPONSE

01

Which names in this list are
familiar to you? Which names
are new?

02

What expectations or hesitations
do you have about studying
these stories and relationships?

HOW TO READ STORIES OF PEOPLE IN THE BIBLE

In this reading plan, we are learning more about the genealogy of Jesus. Here are some principles to keep in mind as you read about the lives of men and women in Jesus's family tree.

ONE

BIBLICAL NARRATIVE IS OFTEN DESCRIPTIVE RATHER THAN PRESCRIPTIVE.

Examples are not always positive or meant to be followed.

TWO

WOMEN AND MEN IN THE BIBLE ARE COMPLEX.

People rarely fall into neat categories of "good" and "bad." Jesus alone is wholly good.

THREE

God spoke into culture as it existed.

OUR SOCIAL NORMS ARE DIFFERENT THAN THOSE WE ENCOUNTER IN THE BIBLE.

It is important to keep in mind that not all practices found in Scripture (e.g., polygamy or slavery) were part of God's design for His creation. At the same time, we remember that, though human laws and customs vary over time, eternal truths remain unchanged.

FOUR

GOD'S REVELATION IS GRADUAL.

Since we have the complete Old and New Testaments, we benefit from knowledge about certain aspects of God's plan that the women and men we read about in Scripture did not.

FIVE

In the Bible,

GOD WORKED THROUGH BROKEN, SINFUL PEOPLE.

(He still does!)

Day 3

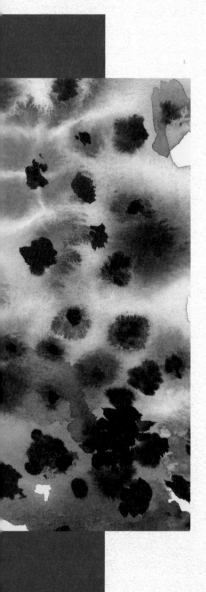

THE FIRST IMAGE-BEARERS

Adam and Eve were the first humans, created in God's image. Placed in God's perfect creation, they were called to be fruitful, multiply, and fill the earth.

GENESIS

FROM CHAPTER 1

²⁶ Then God said, "Let us make man in our image, according to our likeness. They will rule the fish of the sea, the birds of the sky, the livestock, the whole earth, and the creatures that crawl on the earth."

²⁷ So God created man
in his own image;
he created him in the image of God;
he created them male and female.

²⁸ God blessed them, and God said to them, "Be fruitful, multiply, fill the earth, and subdue it. Rule the fish of the sea, the birds of the sky, and every creature that crawls on the earth."

²⁹ God also said, "Look, I have given you every seed-bearing plant on the surface of the entire earth and every tree whose fruit contains seed. This will be food for you, ³⁰ for all the wildlife of the earth, for every bird of the sky, and for every creature that crawls on the earth—everything having the breath of life in it—I have given every green plant for food." And it was so. ³¹ God saw all that he had made, and it was very good indeed. Evening came and then morning: the sixth day.

Man and Woman in the Garden

⁴ These are the records of the heavens and the earth, concerning their creation. At the time that the Lord God made the earth and the heavens, ⁵ no shrub of the field had yet grown on the land, and no plant of the field had yet sprouted, for the Lord God had not made it rain on the land, and there was no man to work the ground. ⁶ But mist would come up from the earth and water all the ground. ⁷ Then the Lord God formed the man out of the dust from the ground and breathed the breath of life into his nostrils, and the man became a living being.

⁸ The Lord God planted a garden in Eden, in the east, and there he placed the man he had formed. ⁹ The Lord God caused to grow out of the ground every tree pleasing in appearance and good for food, including the tree of life in the middle of the garden, as well as the tree of the knowledge of good and evil.

¹⁰ A river went out from Eden to water the garden. From there it divided and became the source of four rivers. ¹¹ The name of the first is Pishon, which flows through the entire land of Havilah, where there is gold. ¹² Gold from that land is pure; bdellium and onyx are also there. ¹³ The name of the second river is Gihon, which flows through the entire land of Cush. ¹⁴ The name of the third river is Tigris, which runs east of Assyria. And the fourth river is the Euphrates.

¹⁵ The Lord God took the man and placed him in the garden of Eden to work it and watch over it. ¹⁶ And the Lord God commanded the man, "You are free to eat from any tree of the garden, ¹⁷ but you must not eat from the tree of the knowledge of good and evil, for on the day you eat from it, you will certainly die." ¹⁸ Then the Lord God said, "It is not good for the man to be alone. I will make a helper corresponding to him." ¹⁹ The Lord God formed out of the ground every wild animal and every bird of the sky, and brought each to the man to see what he would call it. And whatever the man called a living creature, that was its name. ²⁰ The man gave names to all the livestock, to the birds of the sky, and to every wild animal; but for the man no helper was found corresponding to him. ²¹ So the Lord God caused a deep sleep to come over the man, and he slept. God took one of his ribs and closed the flesh at that place. ²² Then the Lord God made the rib he had taken from the man into a woman and brought her to the man. ²³ And the man said:

notes

This one, at last, is bone of my bone
and flesh of my flesh;
this one will be called "woman,"
for she was taken from man.

[24] This is why a man leaves his father and mother and bonds with his wife, and they become one flesh.

[25] Both the man and his wife were naked, yet felt no shame.

RESPONSE

Highlight or underline Genesis 1:26–30, then fill in the blanks below.

GOD MADE THE FIRST HUMANS IN

☐☐☐☐☐☐☐   ☐☐☐☐☐☐☐   ☐☐☐☐☐☐☐

(v. 27).

GOD BLESSED THEM AND TOLD THEM TO

☐☐☐☐☐☐☐   ☐☐☐☐☐☐☐ ,   ☐☐☐☐☐☐☐ ,

☐☐☐☐☐☐☐   ☐☐☐☐☐☐☐   ☐☐☐☐☐☐☐ ,

AND   ☐☐☐☐☐☐☐   ☐☐☐☐☐☐☐   *(v. 28).*

SETH, A SON IN ADAM'S IMAGE

Through Adam and Eve, sin entered the world. Adam's firstborn Cain killed his brother Abel and was left to wander the earth. God provided another son, Seth, to Adam and Eve.

GENESIS

FROM CHAPTER 3

Sin's Consequences

8 Then the man and his wife heard the sound of the LORD God walking in the garden at the time of the evening breeze, and they hid from the LORD God among the trees of the garden. 9 So the LORD God called out to the man and said to him, "Where are you?"

10 And he said, "I heard you in the garden, and I was afraid because I was naked, so I hid."

11 Then he asked, "Who told you that you were naked? Did you eat from the tree that I commanded you not to eat from?"

12 The man replied, "The woman you gave to be with me—she gave me some fruit from the tree, and I ate."

13 So the LORD God asked the woman, "What have you done?"

And the woman said, "The serpent deceived me, and I ate."

¹⁴ So the Lord God said to the serpent:

> Because you have done this,
> you are cursed more than any livestock
> and more than any wild animal.
> You will move on your belly
> and eat dust all the days of your life.
> ¹⁵ I will put hostility between you and the woman,
> and between your offspring and her offspring.
> He will strike your head,
> and you will strike his heel.

¹⁶ He said to the woman:

> I will intensify your labor pains;
> you will bear children with painful effort.
> Your desire will be for your husband,
> yet he will rule over you.

¹⁷ And he said to the man, "Because you listened to your wife and ate from the tree about which I commanded you, 'Do not eat from it':

> The ground is cursed because of you.
> You will eat from it by means of painful labor
> all the days of your life.
> ¹⁸ It will produce thorns and thistles for you,
> and you will eat the plants of the field.
> ¹⁹ You will eat bread by the sweat of your brow
> until you return to the ground,
> since you were taken from it.
> For you are dust,
> and you will return to dust."

²⁰ The man named his wife Eve because she was the mother of all the living. ²¹ The Lord God made clothing from skins for the man and his wife, and he clothed them.

FROM CHAPTER 4

Cain Murders Abel

¹ The man was intimate with his wife Eve, and she conceived and gave birth to Cain. She said, "I have had a male child with the Lord's help." ² She also gave birth to his brother Abel. Now Abel became a shepherd of flocks, but Cain

notes

worked the ground. ³ In the course of time Cain presented some of the land's produce as an offering to the LORD. ⁴ And Abel also presented an offering—some of the firstborn of his flock and their fat portions. The LORD had regard for Abel and his offering, ⁵ but he did not have regard for Cain and his offering. Cain was furious, and he looked despondent.

⁶ Then the LORD said to Cain, "Why are you furious? And why do you look despondent? ⁷ If you do what is right, won't you be accepted? But if you do not do what is right, sin is crouching at the door. Its desire is for you, but you must rule over it."

⁸ Cain said to his brother Abel, "Let's go out to the field." And while they were in the field, Cain attacked his brother Abel and killed him.

⁹ Then the LORD said to Cain, "Where is your brother Abel?"

"I don't know," he replied. "Am I my brother's guardian?"

¹⁰ Then he said, "What have you done? Your brother's blood cries out to me from the ground! ¹¹ So now you are cursed, alienated from the ground that opened its mouth to receive your brother's blood you have shed. ¹² If you work the ground, it will never again give you its yield. You will be a restless wanderer on the earth."

¹³ But Cain answered the LORD, "My punishment is too great to bear! ¹⁴ Since you are banishing me today from the face of the earth, and I must hide from your presence and become a restless wanderer on the earth, whoever finds me will kill me."

¹⁵ Then the LORD replied to him, "In that case, whoever kills Cain will suffer vengeance seven times over." And he placed a mark on Cain so that whoever found him would not kill him. ¹⁶ Then Cain went out from the LORD's presence and lived in the land of Nod, east of Eden.

…

²⁵ Adam was intimate with his wife again, and she gave birth to a son and named him Seth, for she said, "God has given me another offspring in place of Abel, since Cain killed him." ²⁶ A son was born to Seth also, and he named him Enosh. At that time people began to call on the name of the LORD.

FROM CHAPTER 5

The Line of Seth

¹ This is the document containing the family records of Adam. On the day that God created man, he made him in the likeness of God; ² he created them male and female. When they were created, he blessed them and called them mankind.

³ Adam was 130 years old when

he fathered a son in his likeness, according to his image, and named him Seth.

⁴ Adam lived 800 years after he fathered Seth, and he fathered other sons and daughters. ⁵ So Adam's life lasted 930 years; then he died.

RESPONSE

Day 4

For each item listed below, fill in the blanks to create a summary of how the curse affected the original purpose we read yesterday.

THE SERPENT WILL BE _____ *(v. 14)*.

THERE WILL BE _____ BETWEEN THE SERPENT AND THE WOMAN THAT WILL CONTINUE THROUGH HER DESCENDANTS *(v. 15)*.

THE WOMAN'S DESCENDANT WILL ONE DAY _____ _____ _____ *(v. 15)*.

THE WORK AND LABOR OF MEN AND WOMEN, AS WELL AS THEIR RELATIONSHIPS WITH ONE ANOTHER, WILL BE _____ *(HINT: LOOK FOR THE REPEATED WORD IN v. 16 AND v. 17)*.

BECAUSE OF SIN, HUMANS RETURN TO _____ IN DEATH *(v. 19)*. YET ADAM STILL NAMES THE WOMAN EVE, WHICH MEANS _____ _____ _____ _____ *(v. 20)*.

Day 5

NOAH, WHO WALKED WITH GOD

Noah found favor with God when the world was wicked. Though he wasn't perfect, he was obedient to God, following God's instructions to build a boat to preserve creation and his family.

GENESIS

FROM CHAPTER 6

Judgment Decreed

5 When the LORD saw that human wickedness was widespread on the earth and that every inclination of the human mind was nothing but evil all the time, 6 the LORD regretted that he had made man on the earth, and he was deeply grieved. 7 Then the LORD said, "I will wipe mankind, whom I created, off the face of the earth, together with the animals, creatures that crawl, and birds of the sky—for I regret that I made them." 8 Noah, however, found favor with the LORD.

God Warns Noah

9 These are the family records of Noah. Noah was a righteous man, blameless among his contemporaries; Noah walked with God. 10 And Noah fathered three sons: Shem, Ham, and Japheth.

11 Now the earth was corrupt in God's sight, and the earth was filled with wickedness. 12 God saw how corrupt the earth was, for every creature had corrupted its way on the earth. 13 Then God said to Noah, "I have decided to put an end to every creature, for the earth is filled with wickedness because of them; therefore I am going to destroy them along with the earth.

14 "Make yourself an ark of gopher wood. Make rooms in the ark, and cover it with pitch inside and outside. 15 This is how you are to make it: The ark will be 450 feet long, 75 feet wide, and 45 feet high. 16 You are to make a roof, finishing the sides of the ark to within eighteen inches of the roof. You are to put a door in the side of the ark. Make it with lower, middle, and upper decks.

17 "Understand that I am bringing a flood—floodwaters on the earth to destroy every creature under heaven with the breath of life in it. Everything on earth will perish.

[18] But I will establish my covenant with you, and you will enter the ark with your sons, your wife, and your sons' wives. [19] You are also to bring into the ark two of all the living creatures, male and female, to keep them alive with you. [20] Two of everything—from the birds according to their kinds, from the livestock according to their kinds, and from the animals that crawl on the ground according to their kinds—will come to you so that you can keep them alive. [21] Take with you every kind of food that is eaten; gather it as food for you and for them." [22] And Noah did this. He did everything that God had commanded him.

FROM CHAPTER 7

The Flood

[11] In the six hundredth year of Noah's life, in the second month, on the seventeenth day of the month, on that day all the sources of the vast watery depths burst open, the floodgates of the sky were opened, [12] and the rain fell on the earth forty days and forty nights.

FROM CHAPTER 8

[13] In the six hundred first year, in the first month, on the first day of the month, the water that had covered the earth was dried up. Then Noah removed the ark's cover and saw that the surface of the ground was drying. [14] By the twenty-seventh day of the second month, the earth was dry.

The Lord's Promise

[15] Then God spoke to Noah, [16] "Come out of the ark, you, your wife, your sons, and your sons' wives with you.

[17] Bring out all the living creatures that are with you—birds, livestock, those that crawl on the earth—and they will spread over the earth and be fruitful and multiply on the earth."

[18] So Noah, along with his sons, his wife, and his sons' wives, came out. [19] All the animals, all the creatures that crawl, and all the flying creatures—everything that moves on the earth—came out of the ark by their families.

FROM CHAPTER 9

God's Covenant with Noah

[1] God blessed Noah and his sons and said to them, "Be fruitful and multiply and fill the earth. [2] The fear and terror of you will be in every living creature on the earth, every bird of the sky, every creature that crawls on the ground, and all the fish of the sea. They are placed under your authority. [3] Every creature that lives and moves will be food for you; as I gave the green plants, I have given you everything. [4] However, you must not eat meat with its lifeblood in it. [5] And I will require a

notes

penalty for your lifeblood; I will require it from any animal and from any human; if someone murders a fellow human, I will require that person's life.

> [6] Whoever sheds human blood,
> by humans his blood will be shed,
> for God made humans in his image.

[7] But you, be fruitful and multiply; spread out over the earth and multiply on it."

[8] Then God said to Noah and his sons with him, [9] "Understand that I am establishing my covenant with you and your descendants after you, [10] and with every living creature that is with you—birds, livestock, and all wildlife of the earth that are with you—all the animals of the earth that came out of the ark. [11] I establish my covenant with you that never again will every creature be wiped out by floodwaters; there will never again be a flood to destroy the earth."

. . .

[18] Noah's sons who came out of the ark were Shem, Ham, and Japheth. Ham was the father of Canaan. [19] These three were Noah's sons, and from them the whole earth was populated.

FROM CHAPTER 10

The Table of Nations

[1] These are the family records of Noah's sons, Shem, Ham, and Japheth. They also had sons after the flood.

. . .

[21] And Shem, Japheth's older brother, also had sons. Shem was the father of all the sons of Eber. [22] Shem's sons were Elam, Asshur, Arpachshad, Lud, and Aram.

[23] Aram's sons: Uz, Hul, Gether, and Mash.

[24] Arpachshad fathered Shelah, and Shelah fathered Eber. [25] Eber had two sons. One was named Peleg, for during his days the earth was divided; his brother was named Joktan. [26] And Joktan fathered Almodad, Sheleph, Hazarmaveth, Jerah, [27] Hadoram, Uzal, Diklah, [28] Obal, Abimael, Sheba, [29] Ophir, Havilah, and Jobab. All these were Joktan's sons. [30] Their settlements extended from Mesha to Sephar, the eastern hill country.

[31] These are Shem's sons by their clans, according to their languages, in their lands and their nations.

[32] These are the clans of Noah's sons, according to their family records, in their nations. The nations on earth spread out from these after the flood.

01

Reread Genesis 1:26–30 and your notes on Day 3. What similarities do you see in today's reading? (If you're feeling stuck, look at 8:17 and 9:1, 7).

02

In Genesis 9:6, God affirms that all human beings—not just Adam and Eve—are made in His image. What does this mean about our calling as image-bearers?

Keep your reading and work this week in mind as we continue reading over the next four weeks.

GRACE DAY

Take this day to catch up on your reading, pray, and rest in the presence of the Lord.

THEN GOD SAID, "LET US MAKE MAN IN OUR IMAGE, ACCORDING TO OUR LIKENESS. THEY WILL RULE THE FISH OF THE SEA, THE BIRDS OF THE SKY, THE LIVESTOCK, THE WHOLE EARTH, AND THE CREATURES THAT CRAWL ON THE EARTH."

GENESIS 1:26

TRUTH

Day 7

WEEKLY

Scripture is God-breathed and true. When we memorize it,
we carry the good news of Jesus with us wherever we go.

For this reading plan we will work to memorize Romans 8:14-17.
As we are reading through the family line of Jesus, we remember
that we have been adopted into God's family through Jesus.

We'll start by memorizing verse 14.

14 FOR ALL THOSE LED BY GOD'S SPIRIT ARE
GOD'S SONS. 15 FOR YOU DID NOT RECEIVE
A SPIRIT OF SLAVERY TO FALL BACK INTO
FEAR. INSTEAD, YOU RECEIVED THE SPIRIT OF
ADOPTION, BY WHOM WE CRY OUT, "*ABBA*,
FATHER!" 16 THE SPIRIT HIMSELF TESTIFIES
TOGETHER WITH OUR SPIRIT THAT WE ARE
GOD'S CHILDREN, 17 AND IF CHILDREN, ALSO
HEIRS—HEIRS OF GOD AND COHEIRS WITH
CHRIST—IF INDEED WE SUFFER WITH HIM SO
THAT WE MAY ALSO BE GLORIFIED WITH HIM.

ROMANS 8:14–17

See tips for memorizing Scripture on page 172.

THE CALLING OF
THE IMAGE-BEARERS

Scripture documents generation after generation of image-bearers waiting for restoration to the relationship and fullness of the blessing we read on Day 3. Each generation remained in need of the one who would come and crush the serpent's head, someone to begin reversing the curse we summarized on Day 4. Every time our reading includes a person's death, it is a reminder that the ultimate consequences of sin are still in effect. Every birth draws attention to the hope: each new generation of Eve's heirs was a promise that a child would come to set all things right.

AS YOU READ THE STORIES OF MEN AND WOMEN IN THE GENEALOGY OF JESUS, TAKE NOTE OF HOW THE THEMES MENTIONED IN THE ORIGINAL BLESSING AND CURSE WILL COME UP AGAIN AND AGAIN.

Through every story, God's promise of life, restoration, and flourishing remains present.

INHERITANCE

Notice how people look to acquire for themselves blessing and inheritance, and how this relates to what God gives, sustains, and declares to be good.

LEGACY

God called humanity to be fruitful and multiply, filling the earth. Notice in your reading how this desire, and the pain experienced when it is unfulfilled, characterize these stories. Take note of language around infertility, offspring, seed, sons, twins, and lineage.

PLACE

God entrusted all humanity with the stewardship of His creation and the instructions to go out into the earth. Pay attention to God's promise of land. This theme is also present in the marking of special spaces with altars, the creation and maintaining of the tabernacle and temples, and people's desire for a place to be present with God.

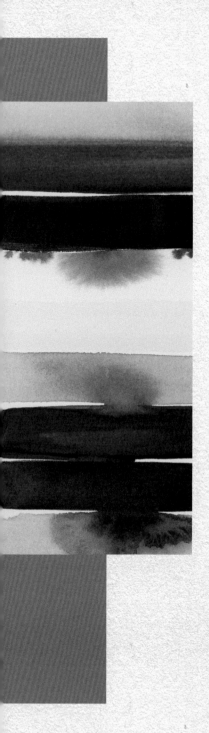

ABRAHAM, SON OF TERAH

God established a covenant with Abraham and his descendents. Abraham's children would be the means by which the entire world would be restored and invited to share in God's redemption blessing. Though Abraham is known for his moments of great faith, he also had moments of doubt in God's promises, expressed in both his words and his actions in trying to create a family line through his own means.

GENESIS

FROM CHAPTER 11

From Shem to Abram

[10] These are the family records of Shem. Shem lived 100 years and fathered Arpachshad two years after the flood. [11] After he fathered Arpachshad, Shem lived 500 years and fathered other sons and daughters. [12] Arpachshad lived 35 years and fathered Shelah. [13] After he fathered Shelah, Arpachshad lived 403 years and fathered other sons and daughters. [14] Shelah lived 30 years and fathered Eber. [15] After he fathered Eber, Shelah lived 403 years and fathered other sons and daughters. [16] Eber lived 34 years and fathered Peleg. [17] After he fathered Peleg, Eber lived 430 years and fathered other sons and daughters. [18] Peleg lived 30 years and fathered Reu. [19] After he fathered Reu, Peleg lived 209 years and fathered other sons and daughters. [20] Reu lived 32 years and fathered Serug. [21] After he fathered Serug, Reu lived 207 years and fathered other sons and daughters. [22] Serug lived 30 years and fathered

WHY THE RITUAL OF CIRCUMCISION?

God promised to make Abraham's descendants into a great nation, one that began in the womb of a barren woman beyond childbearing age (Gn 17:1–8, 17–19). As a reminder of their miraculous origins as a people and a sign of the covenant God made with Abraham, every male was to bear the mark of circumcision (Gn 17:12–14).

Nahor. ²³ After he fathered Nahor, Serug lived 200 years and fathered other sons and daughters. ²⁴ Nahor lived 29 years and fathered Terah. ²⁵ After he fathered Terah, Nahor lived 119 years and fathered other sons and daughters. ²⁶ Terah lived 70 years and fathered Abram, Nahor, and Haran.

²⁷ These are the family records of Terah. Terah fathered Abram, Nahor, and Haran, and Haran fathered Lot. ²⁸ Haran died in his native land, in Ur of the Chaldeans, during his father Terah's lifetime. ²⁹ Abram and Nahor took wives: Abram's wife was named Sarai, and Nahor's wife was named Milcah. She was the daughter of Haran, the father of both Milcah and Iscah. ³⁰ Sarai was unable to conceive; she did not have a child.

³¹ Terah took his son Abram, his grandson Lot (Haran's son), and his daughter-in-law Sarai, his son Abram's wife, and they set out together from Ur of the Chaldeans to go to the land of Canaan. But when they came to Haran, they settled there. ³² Terah lived 205 years and died in Haran.

FROM CHAPTER 12

The Call of Abram

¹ The LORD said to Abram:

Go from your land,
your relatives,
and your father's house
to the land that I will show you.

² I will make you into a great nation,
I will bless you,
I will make your name great,
and you will be a blessing.

³ I will bless those who bless you,
I will curse anyone who treats you with contempt,
and all the peoples on earth
will be blessed through you.

⁴ So Abram went, as the LORD had told him, and Lot went with him. Abram was seventy-five years old when he left Haran. ⁵ He took his wife, Sarai, his nephew Lot, all the possessions they had accumulated, and the people they had acquired in Haran, and they set out for the land of Canaan. When they came to the land of Canaan, ⁶ Abram passed through the land to the site of Shechem, at the oak of Moreh. (At that time the Canaanites were in the land.) ⁷ The LORD appeared to Abram and said, "To your offspring I will give this land." So he built an altar there to the LORD who had appeared to him.

Notes

Notes

The Abrahamic Covenant

[1] After these events, the word of the LORD came to Abram in a vision:

> Do not be afraid, Abram.
> I am your shield;

your reward will be very great.

[2] But Abram said, "Lord GOD, what can you give me, since I am childless and the heir of my house is Eliezer of Damascus?" [3] Abram continued, "Look, you have given me no offspring, so a slave born in my house will be my heir."

[4] Now the word of the LORD came to him: "This one will not be your heir; instead, one who comes from your own body will be your heir." [5] He took him outside and said, "Look at the sky and count the stars, if you are able to count them." Then he said to him, "Your offspring will be that numerous."

[6] Abram believed the LORD, and he credited it to him as righteousness.

[7] He also said to him, "I am the LORD who brought you from Ur of the Chaldeans to give you this land to possess."

[8] But he said, "Lord GOD, how can I know that I will possess it?"

[9] He said to him, "Bring me a three-year-old cow, a three-year-old female goat, a three-year-old ram, a turtledove, and a young pigeon."

[10] So he brought all these to him, cut them in half, and laid the pieces opposite each other, but he did not cut the birds in half. [11] Birds of prey came down on the carcasses, but Abram drove them away. [12] As the sun was setting, a deep sleep came over Abram, and suddenly great terror and darkness descended on him.

[13] Then the LORD said to Abram, "Know this for certain: Your offspring will be resident aliens for four hundred years in a land that does not belong to them and will be enslaved and oppressed. [14] However, I will judge the nation they serve, and afterward they will go out with many possessions. [15] But you will go to your ancestors in peace and be buried at a good old age. [16] In the fourth generation they will return here, for the iniquity of the Amorites has not yet reached its full measure."

[17] When the sun had set and it was dark, a smoking fire pot and a flaming torch appeared and passed between the divided animals. [18] On that day the LORD made a covenant with Abram, saying, "I give this land to your offspring, from the Brook of Egypt to the great river, the Euphrates River: [19] the land of the Kenites,

Kenizzites, Kadmonites, [20] Hethites, Perizzites, Rephaim, [21] Amorites, Canaanites, Girgashites, and Jebusites."

FROM CHAPTER 16

Hagar and Ishmael

[1] Abram's wife, Sarai, had not borne any children for him, but she owned an Egyptian slave named Hagar. [2] Sarai said to Abram, "Since the LORD has prevented me from bearing children, go to my slave; perhaps through her I can build a family." And Abram agreed to what Sarai said. [3] So Abram's wife, Sarai, took Hagar, her Egyptian slave, and gave her to her husband, Abram, as a wife for him. This happened after Abram had lived in the land of Canaan ten years. [4] He slept with Hagar, and she became pregnant. When she saw that she was pregnant, her mistress became contemptible to her. [5] Then Sarai said to Abram, "You are responsible for my suffering! I put my slave in your arms, and when she saw that she was pregnant, I became contemptible to her. May the LORD judge between me and you."

[6] Abram replied to Sarai, "Here, your slave is in your power; do whatever you want with her." Then Sarai mistreated her so much that she ran away from her.

FROM CHAPTER 17

Covenant Circumcision

[1] When Abram was ninety-nine years old, the LORD appeared to him, saying,

"I am God Almighty. Live in my presence and be blameless. [2] I will set up my covenant between me and you, and I will multiply you greatly."

[3] Then Abram fell facedown and God spoke with him: [4] "As for me, here is my covenant with you: You will become the father of many nations. [5] Your name will no longer be Abram; your name will be Abraham, for I will make you the father of many nations. [6] I will make you extremely fruitful and will make nations and kings come from you. [7] I will confirm my covenant that is between me and you and your future offspring throughout their generations. It is a permanent covenant to be your God and the God of your offspring after you. [8] And to you and your future offspring I will give the land where you are residing—all the land of Canaan—as a permanent possession, and I will be their God."

[9] God also said to Abraham, "As for you, you and your offspring after you throughout their generations are to keep my covenant. [10] This is my covenant between me and you and your offspring after you, which you are to keep: Every one of your males must be circumcised. [11] You must circumcise the flesh of your foreskin to serve as a sign of the covenant between me and you."

…

Notes

[17] Abraham fell facedown. Then he laughed and said to himself, "Can a child be born to a hundred-year-old man? Can Sarah, a ninety-year-old woman, give birth?" [18] So Abraham said to God, "If only Ishmael were acceptable to you!"

[19] But God said, "No. Your wife Sarah will bear you a son, and you will name him Isaac. I will confirm my covenant with him as a permanent covenant for his future offspring."

FROM CHAPTER 21

The Birth of Isaac

[1] The LORD came to Sarah as he had said, and the LORD did for Sarah what he had promised. [2] Sarah became pregnant and bore a son to Abraham in his old age, at the appointed time God had told him. [3] Abraham named his son who was born to him—the one Sarah bore to him—Isaac. [4] When his son Isaac was eight days old, Abraham circumcised him, as God had commanded him. [5] Abraham was a hundred years old when his son Isaac was born to him.

[6] Sarah said, "God has made me laugh, and everyone who hears will laugh with me." [7] She also said, "Who would have told Abraham that Sarah would nurse children? Yet I have borne a son for him in his old age."

FROM CHAPTER 25

Abraham's Other Wife and Sons

[1] Abraham had taken another wife, whose name was Keturah, [2] and she bore him Zimran, Jokshan, Medan, Midian, Ishbak, and Shuah. [3] Jokshan fathered Sheba and Dedan. Dedan's sons were the Asshurim, Letushim, and Leummim. [4] And Midian's sons were Ephah, Epher, Hanoch, Abida, and Eldaah. All these were sons of Keturah. [5] Abraham gave everything he owned to Isaac. [6] But Abraham gave gifts to the sons of his concubines, and while he was still alive he sent them eastward, away from his son Isaac, to the land of the East.

Abraham's Death

[7] This is the length of Abraham's life: 175 years. [8] He took his last breath and died at a good old age, old and contented, and he was gathered to his people.

01

What stood out to you or surprised you about Abraham's life?

Though some stories may be familiar, each member of Jesus's genealogy has a complex story with everyday details and moments. Consider the details you may have overlooked or the ways in which their story was different than you remembered or expected.

02

From what you observed, how would you describe Abraham's relationship with God?

We see lives of great faith and lives of disobedience in Jesus's genealogy. No one has followed God perfectly. Consider the ways each person related to, interacted with, and responded to God.

03

What did you relate to in Abraham's story?

Those in the lineage of Jesus were fully human, made in the image of God, with a sin nature just like us. Consider the ways you connect with their faithfulness, their struggles, and God's forgiveness and perseverance.

04

What connections did you see in today's reading to the other stories we've read?

A genealogy is not a record of disparate, individual stories. Instead, it shows the relationship and connection between members of a family. Look for names that you might have otherwise passed over.

ISAAC, WHO NEEDED A SUBSTITUTE

Isaac was the first child of the promised nation through Abraham—the initial fulfillment of God's promise to Abraham to give him a son and an heir. The Lord's provision didn't stop with Isaac's birth. From his wife, Rebekah, to the ram given in his place, the Lord provided for Isaac.

GENESIS

FROM CHAPTER 22

The Sacrifice of Isaac

¹ After these things God tested Abraham and said to him, "Abraham!"

"Here I am," he answered.

² "Take your son," he said, "your only son Isaac, whom you love, go to the land of Moriah, and offer him there as a burnt offering on one of the mountains I will tell you about."

³ So Abraham got up early in the morning, saddled his donkey, and took with him two of his young men and his son Isaac. He split wood for a burnt offering and set out to go to the place God had told him about. ⁴ On the third day Abraham looked up and saw the place in the distance. ⁵ Then Abraham said to his young men, "Stay here with the donkey. The boy and I will go over there to worship; then we'll come back to you." ⁶ Abraham took the wood for the burnt offering and laid it on his son Isaac. In his hand he took the fire and the knife, and the two of them walked on together.

⁷ Then Isaac spoke to his father Abraham and said, "My father."

And he replied, "Here I am, my son."

Isaac said, "The fire and the wood are here, but where is the lamb for the burnt offering?"

⁸ Abraham answered, "God himself will provide the lamb for the burnt offering, my son." Then the two of them walked on together.

⁹ When they arrived at the place that God had told him about, Abraham built the altar there and arranged the wood. He bound his son Isaac and placed him on the altar on top of the wood. ¹⁰ Then Abraham reached out and took the knife to slaughter his son.

¹¹ But the angel of the LORD called to him from heaven and said, "Abraham, Abraham!"

He replied, "Here I am."

¹² Then he said, "Do not lay a hand on the boy or do anything to him. For now I know that you fear God, since you have not withheld your only son from me." ¹³ Abraham looked up and saw a ram caught in the thicket by its horns. So Abraham went and took the ram and offered it as a burnt offering in place of his son. ¹⁴ And Abraham named that place The LORD Will Provide, so today it is said, "It will be provided on the LORD's mountain."

¹⁵ Then the angel of the LORD called to Abraham a second time from heaven ¹⁶ and said, "By myself I have sworn," this

is the LORD's declaration: "Because you have done this thing and have not withheld your only son, [17] I will indeed bless you and make your offspring as numerous as the stars of the sky and the sand on the seashore. Your offspring will possess the city gates of their enemies. [18] And all the nations of the earth will be blessed by your offspring because you have obeyed my command."

FROM CHAPTER 24

A Wife for Isaac

[1] Abraham was now old, getting on in years, and the LORD had blessed him in everything. [2] Abraham said to his servant, the elder of his household who managed all he owned, "Place your hand under my thigh, [3] and I will have you swear by the LORD, God of heaven and God of earth, that you will not take a wife for my son from the daughters of the Canaanites among whom I live, [4] but will go to my land and my family to take a wife for my son Isaac."

…

[10] The servant took ten of his master's camels, and with all kinds of his master's goods in hand, he went to Aram-naharaim, to Nahor's town. [11] At evening, the time when women went out to draw water, he made the camels kneel beside a well outside the town.

[12] "LORD, God of my master Abraham," he prayed, "make this happen for me today, and show kindness to my master Abraham. [13] I am standing here at the spring where the daughters of the men of the town are coming out to draw water. [14] Let the girl to whom I say, 'Please lower your water jug so that I may drink,' and who responds, 'Drink, and I'll water your camels also'—let her be the one you have appointed for your servant Isaac. By this I will know that you have shown kindness to my master."

[15] Before he had finished speaking, there was Rebekah—daughter of Bethuel son of Milcah, the wife of Abraham's brother Nahor—coming with a jug on her shoulder. [16] Now the girl was very beautiful, a virgin—no man had been intimate with her. She went down to the spring, filled her jug, and came up. [17] Then the servant ran to meet her and said, "Please let me have a little water from your jug."

[18] She replied, "Drink, my lord." She quickly lowered her jug to her hand and gave him a drink. [19] When she had finished giving him a drink, she said, "I'll also draw water for your camels until they have had enough to drink." [20] She quickly emptied her jug into the trough and hurried to the well again to draw water. She drew water for all his camels [21] while the man silently watched her to see whether or not the LORD had made his journey a success.

²² As the camels finished drinking, the man took a gold ring weighing half a shekel, and for her wrists two bracelets weighing ten shekels of gold. ²³ "Whose daughter are you?" he asked. "Please tell me, is there room in your father's house for us to spend the night?"

²⁴ She answered him, "I am the daughter of Bethuel son of Milcah, whom she bore to Nahor." ²⁵ She also said to him, "We have plenty of straw and feed and a place to spend the night."

²⁶ Then the man knelt low, worshiped the LORD, ²⁷ and said, "Blessed be the LORD, the God of my master Abraham, who has not withheld his kindness and faithfulness from my master. As for me, the LORD has led me on the journey to the house of my master's relatives."

²⁸ The girl ran and told her mother's household about these things. ²⁹ Now Rebekah had a brother named Laban, and Laban ran out to the man at the spring. ³⁰ As soon as he had seen the ring and the bracelets on his sister's wrists, and when he had heard his sister Rebekah's words—"The man said this to me!"—he went to the man. He was standing there by the camels at the spring.

…

⁵⁸ They called Rebekah and said to her, "Will you go with this man?"

She replied, "I will go." ⁵⁹ So they sent away their sister Rebekah with the one who had nursed and raised her, and Abraham's servant and his men.

⁶⁰ They blessed Rebekah, saying to her:

> Our sister, may you become
> thousands upon ten thousands.
> May your offspring possess
> the city gates of their enemies.

⁶¹ Then Rebekah and her female servants got up, mounted the camels, and followed the man. So the servant took Rebekah and left.

⁶² Now Isaac was returning from Beer-lahai-roi, for he was living in the Negev region. ⁶³ In the early evening Isaac went out to walk in the field, and looking up he saw camels coming. ⁶⁴ Rebekah looked up, and when she saw Isaac, she got down from her camel ⁶⁵ and asked the servant, "Who is that man in the field coming to meet us?"

Notes

The servant answered, "It is my master." So she took her veil and covered herself. [66] Then the servant told Isaac everything he had done.

[67] And Isaac brought her into the tent of his mother Sarah and took Rebekah to be his wife. Isaac loved her, and he was comforted after his mother's death.

FROM CHAPTER 26

The Promise Reaffirmed to Isaac

[1] There was another famine in the land in addition to the one that had occurred in Abraham's time. And Isaac went to Abimelech, king of the Philistines, at Gerar. [2] The LORD appeared to him and said, "Do not go down to Egypt. Live in the land that I tell you about; [3] stay in this land as an alien, and I will be with you and bless you. For I will give all these lands to you and your offspring, and I will confirm the oath that I swore to your father Abraham.

[4] I will make your offspring as numerous as the stars of the sky, I will give your offspring all these lands, and all the nations of the earth will be blessed by your offspring,

[5] because Abraham listened to me and kept my mandate, my commands, my statutes, and my instructions."

...

The Lord Appears to Isaac

[23] From there he went up to Beer-sheba, [24] and the LORD appeared to him that night and said, "I am the God of your father Abraham. Do not be afraid, for I am with you. I will bless you and multiply your offspring because of my servant Abraham."

RESPONSE

01

What stood out to you or
surprised you about Isaac's life?

02

From what you observed,
how would you describe Isaac's
relationship with God?

03

What did you relate to in
Isaac's story?

04

What connections did you see
in today's reading to the other
stories we've read?

GOD THE FATHER

A CATECHISM IS A SERIES OF QUESTIONS AND ANSWERS USED TO TEACH FOUNDATIONAL BELIEFS OF THE CHRISTIAN FAITH.

THE FOLLOWING IS AN EXCERPT FROM THE "GOD THE FATHER" CATECHISM IN THE *BOOK OF COMMON PRAYER*.

Q What do we learn about God as creator from the revelation to Israel?

A *We learn that there is one God, the Father Almighty, creator of heaven and earth, of all that is, seen and unseen.*

Q What does this mean?

A *This means that the universe is good, that it is the work of a single loving God who creates, sustains, and directs it.*

Q What does this mean about our place in the universe?

——

A *It means that the world belongs to its creator; and that we are called to enjoy it and to care for it in accordance with God's purposes.*

Q What does this mean about human life?

——

A *It means that all people are worthy of respect and honor, because all are created in the image of God, and all can respond to the love of God.*

JACOB, HEEL-GRABBER AND INHERITANCE-SNATCHER

Day 10

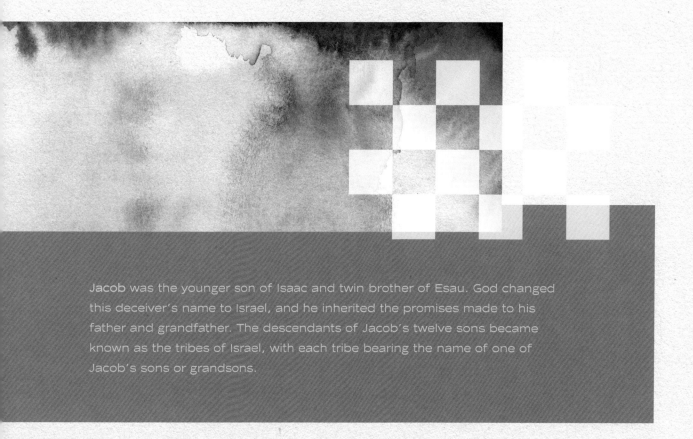

Jacob was the younger son of Isaac and twin brother of Esau. God changed this deceiver's name to Israel, and he inherited the promises made to his father and grandfather. The descendants of Jacob's twelve sons became known as the tribes of Israel, with each tribe bearing the name of one of Jacob's sons or grandsons.

Remember to pay attention to themes of inheritance, legacy, and place throughout your daily reading (p. 46).

GENESIS

FROM CHAPTER 25

²¹ Isaac prayed to the LORD on behalf of his wife because she was childless. The LORD was receptive to his prayer, and his wife Rebekah conceived. ²² But the children inside her struggled with each other, and she said, "Why is this happening to me?" So she went to inquire of the LORD. ²³ And the LORD said to her:

Two nations are in your womb;
two peoples will come from you and be separated.
One people will be stronger than the other,
and the older will serve the younger.

[24] When her time came to give birth, there were indeed twins in her womb. [25] The first one came out red-looking, covered with hair like a fur coat, and they named him Esau. [26] After this, his brother came out grasping Esau's heel with his hand. So he was named Jacob. Isaac was sixty years old when they were born.

Esau Sells His Birthright

[27] When the boys grew up, Esau became an expert hunter, an outdoorsman, but Jacob was a quiet man who stayed at home. [28] Isaac loved Esau because he had a taste for wild game, but Rebekah loved Jacob.

[29] Once when Jacob was cooking a stew, Esau came in from the field exhausted. [30] He said to Jacob, "Let me eat some of that red stuff, because I'm exhausted." That is why he was also named Edom.

[31] Jacob replied, "First sell me your birthright."

[32] "Look," said Esau, "I'm about to die, so what good is a birthright to me?"

[33] Jacob said, "Swear to me first." So he swore to Jacob and sold his birthright to him. [34] Then Jacob gave bread and lentil stew to Esau; he ate, drank, got up, and went away. So Esau despised his birthright.

FROM CHAPTER 26

[34] When Esau was forty years old, he took as his wives Judith daughter of Beeri the Hethite, and Basemath daughter of Elon the Hethite. [35] They made life bitter for Isaac and Rebekah.

FROM CHAPTER 27

The Stolen Blessing

[1] When Isaac was old and his eyes were so weak that he could not see, he called his older son Esau and said to him, "My son."

And he answered, "Here I am."

[2] He said, "Look, I am old and do not know the day of my death. [3] So now take your hunting gear, your quiver and bow, and go out in the field to hunt some game

Notes

for me. [4] Then make me a delicious meal that I love and bring it to me to eat, so that I can bless you before I die."

[5] Now Rebekah was listening to what Isaac said to his son Esau. So while Esau went to the field to hunt some game to bring in, [6] Rebekah said to her son Jacob, "Listen! I heard your father talking with your brother Esau. He said, [7] 'Bring me game and make a delicious meal for me to eat so that I can bless you in the LORD's presence before I die.' [8] Now, my son, listen to me and do what I tell you. [9] Go to the flock and bring me two choice young goats, and I will make them into a delicious meal for your father—the kind he loves. [10] Then take it to your father to eat so that he may bless you before he dies."

[11] Jacob answered Rebekah his mother, "Look, my brother Esau is a hairy man, but I am a man with smooth skin. [12] Suppose my father touches me. Then I will be revealed to him as a deceiver and bring a curse rather than a blessing on myself."

[13] His mother said to him, "Your curse be on me, my son. Just obey me and go get them for me."

[14] So he went and got the goats and brought them to his mother, and his mother made the delicious food his father loved. [15] Then Rebekah took the best clothes of her older son Esau, which were in the house, and had her younger son Jacob wear them. [16] She put the skins of the young goats on his hands and the smooth part of his neck. [17] Then she handed the delicious food and the bread she had made to her son Jacob.

[18] When he came to his father, he said, "My father."

And he answered, "Here I am. Who are you, my son?"

[19] Jacob replied to his father, "I am Esau, your firstborn. I have done as you told me. Please sit up and eat some of my game so that you may bless me."

[20] But Isaac said to his son, "How did you ever find it so quickly, my son?"

He replied, "Because the LORD your God made it happen for me."

[21] Then Isaac said to Jacob, "Please come closer so I can touch you, my son. Are you really my son Esau or not?"

[22] So Jacob came closer to his father Isaac. When he touched him, he said, "The voice is the voice of Jacob, but the hands are the hands of Esau." [23] He did not recognize him, because his hands were hairy like those of his brother Esau; so he blessed him. [24] Again he asked, "Are you really my son Esau?"

And he replied, "I am."

²⁵ Then he said, "Bring it closer to me, and let me eat some of my son's game so that I can bless you." Jacob brought it closer to him, and he ate; he brought him wine, and he drank.

²⁶ Then his father Isaac said to him, "Please come closer and kiss me, my son." ²⁷ So he came closer and kissed him.

...

³⁰ As soon as Isaac had finished blessing Jacob and Jacob had left the presence of his father Isaac, his brother Esau arrived from his hunting. ³¹ He had also made some delicious food and brought it to his father. He said to his father, "Let my father get up and eat some of his son's game, so that you may bless me."

³² But his father Isaac said to him, "Who are you?"

He answered, "I am Esau your firstborn son."

³³ Isaac began to tremble uncontrollably. "Who was it then," he said, "who hunted game and brought it to me? I ate it all before you came in, and I blessed him. Indeed, he will be blessed!"

³⁴ When Esau heard his father's words, he cried out with a loud and bitter cry and said to his father, "Bless me too, my father!"

³⁵ But he replied, "Your brother came deceitfully and took your blessing."

³⁶ So he said, "Isn't he rightly named Jacob? For he has cheated me twice now. He took my birthright, and look, now he has taken my blessing."

...

Esau's Anger

⁴¹ Esau held a grudge against Jacob because of the blessing his father had given him. And Esau determined in his heart, "The days of mourning for my father are approaching; then I will kill my brother Jacob."

⁴² When the words of her older son Esau were reported to Rebekah, she summoned her younger son Jacob and said to him, "Listen, your brother Esau is consoling himself by planning to kill you. ⁴³ So now, my son, listen to me. Flee at once to my brother Laban in Haran, ⁴⁴ and stay with him for a few days until your brother's anger subsides— ⁴⁵ until your brother's rage turns away from you and he forgets what you have done to him. Then I will send for you

Notes

and bring you back from there. Why should I lose you both in one day?"

⁴⁶ So Rebekah said to Isaac, "I'm sick of my life because of these Hethite girls. If Jacob marries someone from around here, like these Hethite girls, what good is my life?"

FROM CHAPTER 28

¹ So Isaac summoned Jacob, blessed him, and commanded him, "Do not marry a Canaanite girl. ² Go at once to Paddan-aram, to the house of Bethuel, your mother's father. Marry one of the daughters of Laban, your mother's brother. ³ May God Almighty bless you and make you fruitful and multiply you so that you become an assembly of peoples. ⁴ May God give you and your offspring the blessing of Abraham so that you may possess the land where you live as a foreigner, the land God gave to Abraham." ⁵ So Isaac sent Jacob to Paddan-aram, to Laban son of Bethuel the Aramean, the brother of Rebekah, the mother of Jacob and Esau.

…

Jacob at Bethel

¹⁰ Jacob left Beer-sheba and went toward Haran. ¹¹ He reached a certain place and spent the night there because the sun had set. He took one of the stones from the place, put it there at his head, and lay down in that place. ¹² And he dreamed: A stairway was set on the ground with its top reaching the sky, and God's angels were going up and down on it. ¹³ The LORD was standing there beside him, saying, "I am the LORD, the God of your father Abraham and the God of Isaac. I will give you and your offspring the land on which you are lying. ¹⁴ Your offspring will be like the dust of the earth, and you will spread out toward the west, the east, the north, and the south. All the peoples on earth will be blessed through you and your offspring. ¹⁵ Look, I am with you and will watch over you wherever you go. I will bring you back to this land, for I will not leave you until I have done what I have promised you."

FROM CHAPTER 35

⁹ God appeared to Jacob again after he returned from Paddan-aram, and he blessed him. ¹⁰ God said to him, "Your name is Jacob; you will no longer be named Jacob, but your name will be Israel." So he named him Israel. ¹¹ God also said to him, "I am God Almighty. Be fruitful and multiply. A nation, indeed an assembly of nations, will come from you, and kings will descend from you. ¹² I will give to you the land that I gave to Abraham and Isaac. And I will give the land to your future descendants." ¹³ Then God withdrew from him at the place where he had spoken to him.

…

Israel's Sons

²² …Jacob had twelve sons:

²³ Leah's sons were Reuben (Jacob's firstborn),
Simeon, Levi, Judah,
Issachar, and Zebulun.
²⁴ Rachel's sons were
Joseph and Benjamin.
²⁵ The sons of Rachel's slave Bilhah
were Dan and Naphtali.
²⁶ The sons of Leah's slave Zilpah
were Gad and Asher.

These are the sons of Jacob, who were born to him in Paddan-aram.

01

What stood out to you or
surprised you about Jacob's life?

02

From what you observed,
how would you describe Jacob's
relationship with God?

03

What did you relate to in
Jacob's story?

04

What connections did you see
in today's reading to the other
stories we've read?

JUDAH, HIS BROTHERS' KEEPER

Judah was the fourth son of Jacob. He proposed that they sell their brother Joseph into slavery rather than killing him, a decision that resulted in Joseph being separated from his family for more than twenty years. When Joseph tested his brothers in Egypt, Judah offered his own life to protect his younger brother Benjamin. The tribe that descended from Judah eventually came to represent the whole of the nation of Israel.

GENESIS

FROM CHAPTER 29

Jacob's Sons

³¹ When the LORD saw that Leah was neglected, he opened her womb; but Rachel was unable to conceive.

…

³⁵ And she conceived again, gave birth to a son, and said, "This time I will praise the LORD." Therefore she named him Judah. Then Leah stopped having children.

FROM CHAPTER 37

¹ Jacob lived in the land where his father had stayed, the land of Canaan. ² These are the family records of Jacob.

At seventeen years of age, Joseph tended sheep with his brothers. The young man was working with the sons of Bilhah and Zilpah, his father's wives, and he brought a bad report about them to their father.

³ Now Israel loved Joseph more than his other sons because Joseph was a son born to him in his old age, and he made a long-sleeved robe for him. ⁴ When his brothers saw that their father loved him more than all his brothers, they hated him and could not bring themselves to speak peaceably to him.

⁵ Then Joseph had a dream. When he told it to his brothers, they hated him even more.

…

¹⁴ Then Israel said to him, "Go and see how your brothers and the flocks are doing, and bring word back to me." So he sent him from the Hebron Valley, and he went to Shechem.

…

[18] They saw him in the distance, and before he had reached them, they plotted to kill him. [19] They said to one another, "Oh, look, here comes that dream expert! [20] So now, come on, let's kill him and throw him into one of the pits. We can say that a vicious animal ate him. Then we'll see what becomes of his dreams!"

...

[23] When Joseph came to his brothers, they stripped off Joseph's robe, the long-sleeved robe that he had on. [24] Then they took him and threw him into the pit. The pit was empty, without water.

[25] They sat down to eat a meal, and when they looked up, there was a caravan of Ishmaelites coming from Gilead. Their camels were carrying aromatic gum, balsam, and resin, going down to Egypt.

[26] Judah said to his brothers, "What do we gain if we kill our brother and cover up his blood? [27] Come on, let's sell him to the Ishmaelites and not lay a hand on him, for he is our brother, our own flesh," and his brothers agreed. [28] When Midianite traders passed by, his brothers pulled Joseph out of the pit and sold him for twenty pieces of silver to the Ishmaelites, who took Joseph to Egypt.

FROM CHAPTER 41

[46] Joseph was thirty years old when he entered the service of Pharaoh king of Egypt. Joseph left Pharaoh's presence and traveled throughout the land of Egypt.

...

[55] When the whole land of Egypt was stricken with famine, the people cried out to Pharaoh for food. Pharaoh told all Egypt, "Go to Joseph and do whatever he tells you."

...

[57] Every land came to Joseph in Egypt to buy grain, for the famine was severe in every land.

FROM CHAPTER 42

[5] The sons of Israel were among those who came to buy grain, for the famine was in the land of Canaan. [6] Joseph was in charge of the country; he sold grain to all its people. His brothers came and bowed down before him with their faces to the ground. [7] When Joseph saw his brothers, he recognized them, but he treated them like strangers and spoke harshly to them.

"Where do you come from?" he asked.

"From the land of Canaan to buy food," they replied.

Notes

[8] Although Joseph recognized his brothers, they did not recognize him. [9] Joseph remembered his dreams about them and said to them, "You are spies. You have come to see the weakness of the land."

[10] "No, my lord. Your servants have come to buy food," they said. [11] "We are all sons of one man. We are honest; your servants are not spies."

[12] "No," he said to them. "You have come to see the weakness of the land."

[13] But they replied, "We, your servants, were twelve brothers, the sons of one man in the land of Canaan. The youngest is now with our father, and one is no longer living."

[14] Then Joseph said to them, "I have spoken: 'You are spies!'"

…

[20] Bring your youngest brother to me so that your words can be confirmed; then you won't die." And they consented to this.

[21] Then they said to each other, "Obviously, we are being punished for what we did to our brother. We saw his deep distress when he pleaded with us, but we would not listen. That is why this trouble has come to us."

FROM CHAPTER 43

Decision to Return to Egypt

[1] Now the famine in the land was severe. [2] When they had used up the grain they had brought back from Egypt, their father said to them, "Go back and buy us a little food."

[3] But Judah said to him, "The man specifically warned us, 'You will not see me again unless your brother is with you.' [4] If you will send our brother with us, we will go down and buy food for you. [5] But if you will not send him, we will not go, for the man said to us, 'You will not see me again unless your brother is with you.'"

[6] "Why have you caused me so much trouble?" Israel asked. "Why did you tell the man that you had another brother?"

[7] They answered, "The man kept asking about us and our family: 'Is your father still alive? Do you have another brother?' And we answered him accordingly. How could we know that he would say, 'Bring your brother here'?"

[8] Then Judah said to his father Israel, "Send the boy with me. We will be on our way so that we may live and not die—neither we, nor you, nor our dependents.

⁹ I will be responsible for him. You can hold me personally accountable! If I do not bring him back to you and set him before you, I will be guilty before you forever."

…

¹⁵ The men took this gift, double the amount of silver, and Benjamin. They immediately went down to Egypt and stood before Joseph.

…

²⁹ When he looked up and saw his brother Benjamin, his mother's son, he asked, "Is this your youngest brother that you told me about?" Then he said, "May God be gracious to you, my son." ³⁰ Joseph hurried out because he was overcome with emotion for his brother, and he was about to weep. He went into an inner room and wept there. ³¹ Then he washed his face and came out. Regaining his composure, he said, "Serve the meal."

…

³³ They were seated before him in order by age, from the firstborn to the youngest. The men looked at each other in astonishment. ³⁴ Portions were served to them from Joseph's table, and Benjamin's portion was five times larger than any of theirs. They drank and became drunk with Joseph.

FROM CHAPTER 44

¹ Joseph commanded his steward, "Fill the men's bags with as much food as they can carry, and put each one's silver at the top of his bag. ² Put my cup, the silver one, at the top of the youngest one's bag, along with the silver for his grain." So he did as Joseph told him.

³ At morning light, the men were sent off with their donkeys. ⁴ They had not gone very far from the city when Joseph said to his steward, "Get up. Pursue the men, and when you overtake them, say to them, 'Why have you repaid evil for good? ⁵ Isn't this the cup that my master drinks from and uses for divination? What you have done is wrong!'"

…

¹⁴ When Judah and his brothers reached Joseph's house, he was still there. They fell to the ground before him. ¹⁵ "What have you done?" Joseph said to them. "Didn't you know that a man like me could uncover the truth by divination?"

¹⁶ "What can we say to my lord?" Judah replied. "How can we plead? How can we justify ourselves? God has exposed your servants' iniquity. We are now my lord's slaves—both we and the one in whose possession the cup was found."

[17] Then Joseph said, "I swear that I will not do this. The man in whose possession the cup was found will be my slave. The rest of you can go in peace to your father."

Judah's Plea for Benjamin

[18] But Judah approached him and said, "My lord, please let your servant speak personally to my lord. Do not be angry with your servant, for you are like Pharaoh. [19] My lord asked his servants, 'Do you have a father or a brother?' [20] and we answered my lord, 'We have an elderly father and a younger brother, the child of his old age. The boy's brother is dead. He is the only one of his mother's sons left, and his father loves him.' [21] Then you said to your servants, 'Bring him to me so that I can see him.' [22] But we said to my lord, 'The boy cannot leave his father. If he were to leave, his father would die.' [23] Then you said to your servants, 'If your younger brother does not come down with you, you will not see me again.'

[24] "This is what happened when we went back to your servant my father: We reported to him the words of my lord. [25] But our father said, 'Go again, and buy us a little food.' [26] We told him, 'We cannot go down unless our younger brother goes with us. If our younger brother isn't with us, we cannot see the man.' [27] Your servant my father said to us, 'You know that my wife bore me two sons. [28] One is gone from me—I said he must have been torn to pieces—and I have never seen him again. [29] If you also take this one from me and anything happens to him, you will bring my gray hairs down to Sheol in sorrow.'

[30] "So if I come to your servant my father and the boy is not with us—his life is wrapped up with the boy's life— [31] when he sees that the boy is not with us, he will die. Then your servants will have brought the gray hairs of your servant our father down to Sheol in sorrow. [32] Your servant became accountable to my father for the boy, saying, 'If I do not return him to you, I will always bear the guilt for sinning against you, my father.' [33] Now please let your servant remain here as my lord's slave, in place of the boy. Let him go back with his brothers. [34] For how can I go back to my father without the boy? I could not bear to see the grief that would overwhelm my father."

FROM CHAPTER 45

[4] Then Joseph said to his brothers, "Please, come near me," and they came near. "I am Joseph, your brother," he said, "the one you sold into Egypt. [5] And now don't be grieved or angry with yourselves for selling me here, because God sent me ahead of you to preserve life. [6] For the famine has been in the land these two years, and there will be five more years without plowing or harvesting. [7] God sent me ahead of you to establish you as a remnant within the land and to keep you alive by a great deliverance. [8] Therefore it was not you who sent me here, but God. He has made me a father to Pharaoh, lord of his entire household, and ruler over all the land of Egypt.

[9] "Return quickly to my father and say to him, 'This is what your son Joseph says: "God has made me lord of all Egypt. Come down to me without delay. [10] You can settle in the land of Goshen and be near me—you, your children, and your grandchildren, your flocks, your herds, and all you have."'"

FROM CHAPTER 49

[8] Judah, your brothers will praise you.
Your hand will be on the necks of your enemies;
your father's sons will bow down to you.
[9] Judah is a young lion—
my son, you return from the kill.
He crouches; he lies down like a lion
or a lioness—who dares to rouse him?
[10] The scepter will not depart from Judah
or the staff from between his feet
until he whose right it is comes
and the obedience of the peoples belongs to him.

RESPONSE

01

What stood out to you or
surprised you about Judah's life?

02

From what you observed,
how would you describe Judah's
relationship with God?

03

What did you relate to in
Judah's story?

04

What connections did you see
in today's reading to the other
stories we've read?

TAMAR, WHO VEILED HER FACE

Tamar was the Canaanite daughter-in-law of Judah whose husband was put to death. After Judah's son passed away, Judah neglected a command found in the Mosaic law and failed to provide a husband with whom Tamar could have a child. To have a child through her deceased husband's family line, Tamar dressed as a prostitute and slept with Judah, which led to twin sons.

GENESIS

FROM CHAPTER 38

Judah and Tamar

¹ At that time Judah left his brothers and settled near an Adullamite named Hirah. ² There Judah saw the daughter of a Canaanite named Shua; he took her as a wife and slept with her. ³ She conceived and gave birth to a son, and he named him Er. ⁴ She conceived again, gave birth to a son, and named him Onan. ⁵ She gave birth to another son and named him Shelah. It was at Chezib that she gave birth to him.

⁶ Judah got a wife for Er, his firstborn, and her name was Tamar. ⁷ Now Er, Judah's firstborn, was evil in the Lord's sight, and the Lord put him to death. ⁸ Then Judah said to Onan, "Sleep with your brother's wife. Perform your duty as her brother-in-law and produce offspring for your brother." ⁹ But Onan knew that the offspring would not be his, so whenever he slept with his brother's wife, he released his semen on the ground so that he would not produce offspring for his brother. ¹⁰ What he did was evil in the Lord's sight, so he put him to death also.

¹¹ Then Judah said to his daughter-in-law Tamar, "Remain a widow in your father's house until my son Shelah grows up." For he thought, "He might die too, like his brothers." So Tamar went to live in her father's house.

¹² After a long time Judah's wife, the daughter of Shua, died. When Judah had finished mourning, he and his friend Hirah the Adullamite went up to Timnah to his sheepshearers. ¹³ Tamar was told, "Your father-in-law is going up to Timnah to shear his sheep." ¹⁴ So she took off her widow's clothes, veiled her face, covered herself, and sat at the entrance to Enaim, which is on the way to Timnah. For she saw that, though Shelah had grown up, she had not been given to him as a wife. ¹⁵ When Judah saw her, he thought she was a prostitute, for she had covered her face.

¹⁶ He went over to her and said, "Come, let me sleep with you," for he did not know that she was his daughter-in-law.

She said, "What will you give me for sleeping with me?"

¹⁷ "I will send you a young goat from my flock," he replied.

But she said, "Only if you leave something with me until you send it."

¹⁸ "What should I give you?" he asked.

She answered, "Your signet ring, your cord, and the staff in your hand." So he gave them to her and slept with her, and she became pregnant by him. [19] She got up and left, then removed her veil and put her widow's clothes back on.

[20] When Judah sent the young goat by his friend the Adullamite in order to get back the items he had left with the woman, he could not find her. [21] He asked the men of the place, "Where is the cult prostitute who was beside the road at Enaim?"

"There has been no cult prostitute here," they answered.

[22] So the Adullamite returned to Judah, saying, "I couldn't find her, and besides, the men of the place said, 'There has been no cult prostitute here.'"

[23] Judah replied, "Let her keep the items for herself; otherwise we will become a laughingstock. After all, I did send this young goat, but you couldn't find her."

[24] About three months later Judah was told, "Your daughter-in-law, Tamar, has been acting like a prostitute, and now she is pregnant."

"Bring her out," Judah said, "and let her be burned to death!"

[25] As she was being brought out, she sent her father-in-law this message: "I am pregnant by the man to whom these items belong." And she added, "Examine them. Whose signet ring, cord, and staff are these?"

[26] Judah recognized them and said, "She is more in the right than I, since I did not give her to my son Shelah." And he did not know her intimately again.

[27] When the time came for her to give birth, there were twins in her womb.

[28] As she was giving birth, one of them put out his hand, and the midwife took it and tied a scarlet thread around it, announcing, "This one came out first." [29] But then he pulled his hand back, out came his brother, and she said, "What a breakout you have made for yourself!" So he was named Perez. [30] Then his brother, who had the scarlet thread tied to his hand, came out, and was named Zerah.

RESPONSE

01

What stood out to you or
surprised you about Tamar's life?

02

From what you observed,
how would you describe Tamar's
relationship with God?

03

What did you relate to in
Tamar's story?

04

What connections did you see
in today's reading to the other
stories we've read?

GRACE DAY

Take this day to catch up on your reading, pray, and rest in the presence of the Lord.

"*I WILL MAKE YOU INTO A GREAT NATION,*

I WILL BLESS YOU,

I WILL MAKE YOUR NAME GREAT,

AND YOU WILL BE A BLESSING.

I WILL BLESS THOSE WHO BLESS YOU,

I WILL CURSE ANYONE WHO TREATS YOU

* WITH CONTEMPT,*

AND ALL THE PEOPLES ON EARTH

WILL BE BLESSED THROUGH YOU."

GENESIS 12:2-3

WEEKLY  TRUTH

Day 14

Scripture is God-breathed and true. When we memorize it, we carry the good news of Jesus with us wherever we go.

For this reading plan we are working to memorize Romans 8:14–17. Let's continue by adding verse 15, a reminder of the access we have to God as His children.

[14] FOR ALL THOSE LED BY GOD'S SPIRIT ARE GOD'S SONS. [15] FOR YOU DID NOT RECEIVE A SPIRIT OF SLAVERY TO FALL BACK INTO FEAR. INSTEAD, YOU RECEIVED THE SPIRIT OF ADOPTION, BY WHOM WE CRY OUT, "*ABBA, FATHER!*" [16] THE SPIRIT HIMSELF TESTIFIES TOGETHER WITH OUR SPIRIT THAT WE ARE GOD'S CHILDREN, [17] AND IF CHILDREN, ALSO HEIRS—HEIRS OF GOD AND COHEIRS WITH CHRIST—IF INDEED WE SUFFER WITH HIM SO THAT WE MAY ALSO BE GLORIFIED WITH HIM.

ROMANS 8:14–17

See tips for memorizing Scripture on page 172.

NAHSHON, WHO BROUGHT THE FIRST OFFERING

Nahshon was the brother-in-law of Aaron and the leader of the tribe of Judah. He was part of the generation that was enslaved in Egypt, escaped in the exodus, experienced God's revelation at Mount Sinai, and died during the desert wanderings.

GENESIS

FROM CHAPTER 46

¹ Israel set out with all that he had and came to Beer-sheba, and he offered sacrifices to the God of his father Isaac. ² That night God spoke to Israel in a vision: "Jacob, Jacob!" he said.

And Jacob replied, "Here I am."

³ God said, "I am God, the God of your father. Do not be afraid to go down to Egypt, for I will make you into a great nation there. ⁴ I will go down with you to Egypt, and I will also bring you back. Joseph will close your eyes when you die."

⁵ Jacob left Beer-sheba. The sons of Israel took their father Jacob in the wagons Pharaoh had sent to carry him, along with their dependents and their wives. ⁶ They also took their cattle and possessions they had acquired in the land of Canaan.

Then Jacob and all his offspring with him came to Egypt. ⁷ His sons and grandsons, his daughters and granddaughters, indeed all his offspring, he brought with him to Egypt.

EXODUS

FROM CHAPTER 1

⁵ The total number of Jacob's descendants was seventy; Joseph was already in Egypt.

⁶ Joseph and all his brothers and all that generation eventually died.

⁷ But the Israelites were fruitful, increased rapidly, multiplied,

and became extremely numerous so that the land was filled with them.

⁸ A new king, who did not know about Joseph, came to power in Egypt. ⁹ He said to his people, "Look, the Israelite people are more numerous and powerful than we are. ¹⁰ Come, let's deal shrewdly with them; otherwise they will multiply further, and when war breaks out, they will join our enemies, fight against us, and leave the country." ¹¹ So the Egyptians assigned taskmasters over the Israelites to oppress them with forced labor. They built Pithom and Rameses as supply cities for Pharaoh. ¹² But the more they oppressed them, the more they multiplied and spread so that the Egyptians came to dread the Israelites.

FROM CHAPTER 3

⁷ Then the LORD said, "I have observed the misery of my people in Egypt, and have heard them crying out because of their oppressors. I know about their sufferings, ⁸ and I have come down to rescue them from the power of the Egyptians and to bring them from that land to a good and spacious land, a land flowing with milk and honey—the territory of the Canaanites, Hethites, Amorites, Perizzites, Hivites, and Jebusites. ⁹ So because the Israelites' cry for help has come to me, and I have also seen the way the Egyptians are oppressing them,¹⁰ therefore, go. I am sending you to Pharaoh so that you may lead my people, the Israelites, out of Egypt."

¹¹ But Moses asked God, "Who am I that I should go to Pharaoh and that I should bring the Israelites out of Egypt?"

FROM CHAPTER 4

¹⁰ But Moses replied to the LORD, "Please, Lord, I have never been eloquent—either in the past or recently or since you have been speaking to your servant—because my mouth and my tongue are sluggish."

¹¹ The LORD said to him, "Who placed a mouth on humans? Who makes a person mute or deaf, seeing or blind? Is it not I, the LORD? ¹² Now go! I will help you speak and I will teach you what to say."

¹³ Moses said, "Please, Lord, send someone else."

¹⁴ Then the LORD's anger burned against Moses, and he said, "Isn't Aaron the Levite your brother? I know that he can speak well. And also, he is on his way now to meet you. He will rejoice when he sees you. ¹⁵ You will speak with him and tell him what to say. I will help both you and him to speak and will teach you both what to do. ¹⁶ He will speak to the people for you. He will serve as a mouth for you, and you will serve as God to him. ¹⁷ And take this staff in your hand that you will perform the signs with."

FROM CHAPTER 6

²³ Aaron married Elisheba,
daughter of Amminadab and sister of Nahshon.
She bore him Nadab and Abihu, Eleazar and Ithamar.

. . .

²⁶ It was this Aaron and Moses whom the LORD told, "Bring the Israelites out of the land of Egypt according to their military divisions."

FROM CHAPTER 12

²¹ Then Moses summoned all the elders of Israel and said to them, "Go, select an animal from the flock according to your families, and slaughter the Passover animal. ²² Take a cluster of hyssop, dip it in the blood that is in the basin, and brush the lintel and the two doorposts with some of the blood in

the basin. None of you may go out the door of his house until morning. ²³ When the LORD passes through to strike Egypt and sees the blood on the lintel and the two doorposts, he will pass over the door and not let the destroyer enter your houses to strike you."

…

The Exodus

²⁹ Now at midnight the LORD struck every firstborn male in the land of Egypt, from the firstborn of Pharaoh who sat on his throne to the firstborn of the prisoner who was in the dungeon, and every firstborn of the livestock. ³⁰ During the night Pharaoh got up, he along with all his officials and all the Egyptians, and there was a loud wailing throughout Egypt because there wasn't a house without someone dead. ³¹ He summoned Moses and Aaron during the night and said, "Get out immediately from among my people, both you and the Israelites, and go, worship the LORD as you have said. ³² Take even your flocks and your herds as you asked and leave, and also bless me."

³³ Now the Egyptians pressured the people in order to send them quickly out of the country, for they said, "We're all going to die!" ³⁴ So the people took their dough before it was leavened, with their kneading bowls wrapped up in their clothes on their shoulders.

³⁵ The Israelites acted on Moses's word and asked the Egyptians for silver and gold items and for clothing. ³⁶ And the LORD gave the people such favor with the Egyptians that they gave them what they requested. In this way they plundered the Egyptians.

…

⁴⁰ The time that the Israelites lived in Egypt was 430 years. ⁴¹ At the end of 430 years, on that same day, all the LORD's military divisions went out from the land of Egypt.

NUMBERS

FROM CHAPTER 7

Offerings from the Leaders

¹ On the day Moses finished setting up the tabernacle, he anointed and consecrated it and all its furnishings, along with the altar and all its utensils. After he anointed and consecrated these things, ² the leaders of Israel, the heads of their ancestral families, presented an offering. They were the tribal leaders who supervised the registration. ³ They brought as their offering before the LORD six covered carts and twelve oxen, a cart from every two leaders and an ox from each one, and presented them in front of the tabernacle.

⁴ The LORD said to Moses, ⁵ "Accept these from them to be used in the work of the tent of meeting, and give this offering to the Levites, to each division according to their service."

⁶ So Moses took the carts and oxen and gave them to the Levites. ⁷ He gave the Gershonites two carts and four oxen corresponding to their service, ⁸ and gave the Merarites four carts and eight oxen corresponding to their service, under the direction of Ithamar son of Aaron the priest. ⁹ But he did not give any to the Kohathites, since their responsibility was service related to the holy objects carried on their shoulders.

¹⁰ The leaders also presented the dedication gift for the altar when it was anointed. The leaders presented their offerings in front of the altar. ¹¹ The LORD told Moses, "Each day have one leader present his offering for the dedication of the altar."

¹² The one who presented his offering on the first day was Nahshon son of Amminadab from the tribe of Judah. ¹³ His offering was one silver dish weighing 3¼ pounds and one silver basin weighing 1¾ pounds, measured by the standard sanctuary shekel, both of them full of fine flour mixed with oil for a grain offering; ¹⁴ one gold bowl weighing four ounces, full of incense; ¹⁵ one young bull, one ram, and one male lamb a year old, for a burnt offering; ¹⁶ one male goat for a sin offering; ¹⁷ and two bulls, five rams, five male goats, and five male lambs a year old, for the fellowship sacrifice. This was the offering of Nahshon son of Amminadab.

01

_____

What stood out to you or surprised you about Nahshon's life?

02

_____

From what you observed, how would you describe Nahshon's relationship with God?

03

_____

What did you relate to in Nahshon's story?

04

_____

What connections did you see in today's reading to the other stories we've read?

RAHAB, WHO ASKED TO BELONG

As the Israelites were preparing to enter into the promised land after wandering in the desert, **Rahab** was a Canaanite woman in Jericho who hid the Israelite spies planning to conquer the city. Her loyalty to God was rewarded with a place and protection among God's people, even though she was an outsider.

JOSHUA

FROM CHAPTER 1

¹ After the death of Moses the LORD's servant, the LORD spoke to Joshua son of Nun, Moses's assistant: ² "Moses my servant is dead. Now you and all the people prepare to cross over the Jordan to the land I am giving the Israelites. ³ I have given you every place where the sole of your foot treads, just as I promised Moses. ⁴ Your territory will be from the wilderness and Lebanon to the great river, the Euphrates River—all the land of the Hittites—and west to the Mediterranean Sea. ⁵ No one will be able to stand against you as long as you live. I will be with you, just as I was with Moses. I will not leave you or abandon you.

⁶ "Be strong and courageous, for

you will distribute the land I swore to their ancestors to give them as an inheritance.

⁷ Above all, be strong and very courageous to observe carefully the whole instruction my servant Moses commanded you. Do not turn from it to the right or the left, so that you will have success wherever you go. ⁸ This book of instruction must not depart from your mouth; you are to meditate on it day and night so that you may carefully observe everything written in it. For then you will prosper and succeed in whatever you do. ⁹ Haven't I commanded you: be strong and courageous? Do not be afraid or discouraged, for the LORD your God is with you wherever you go."

FROM CHAPTER 2

Spies Sent to Jericho

¹ Joshua son of Nun secretly sent two men as spies from the Acacia Grove, saying, "Go and scout the land, especially Jericho." So they left, and they came to the house of a prostitute named Rahab, and stayed there.

² The king of Jericho was told, "Look, some of the Israelite men have come here tonight to investigate the land." ³ Then the king of Jericho sent word to Rahab and said, "Bring out the men who came to you and entered your house, for they came to investigate the entire land."

⁴ But the woman had taken the two men and hidden them. So she said, "Yes, the men did come to me, but I didn't know where they were from. ⁵ At nightfall, when the city gate was about to close, the men went out, and I don't know where they were going. Chase after them quickly, and you can catch up with them!" ⁶ But she had taken them up to the roof and hidden them among the stalks of flax that she had arranged on the roof. ⁷ The men pursued them along the road to the fords of the Jordan, and as soon as they left to pursue them, the city gate was shut.

The Promise to Rahab

⁸ Before the men fell asleep, she went up on the roof ⁹ and said to them, "I know that the LORD has given you this land and that the terror of you has fallen on us, and everyone who lives in the land is panicking because of you. ¹⁰ For we have heard how the LORD dried up the water of the Red Sea before you when you came out of Egypt, and what you did to Sihon and Og, the two Amorite kings you completely destroyed across the Jordan. ¹¹ When we heard this, we lost heart, and everyone's courage failed because of you, for the LORD your God is God in heaven above and on earth below. ¹² Now please swear to me by the LORD that you will also show kindness to my father's family, because I showed kindness to you. Give me a sure sign ¹³ that you will spare the lives of my father, mother, brothers, sisters, and all who belong to them, and save us from death."

¹⁴ The men answered her, "We will give our lives for yours. If you don't report our mission, we will show kindness and faithfulness to you when the LORD gives us the land."

¹⁵ Then she let them down by a rope through the window, since she lived in a house that was built into the wall of the city. ¹⁶ "Go to the hill country so that the men pursuing you won't find you," she said to them. "Hide there for three days until they return; afterward, go on your way."

¹⁷ The men said to her, "We will be free from this oath you made us swear, ¹⁸ unless, when we enter the land, you tie this scarlet cord to the window through which you let us down. Bring your father, mother, brothers, and all your father's family into your house. ¹⁹ If anyone goes out the doors of your house, his death will be his own fault, and we will be innocent. But if anyone with you in the house should be harmed, his death will be our fault. ²⁰ And if you report our mission, we are free from the oath you made us swear."

²¹ "Let it be as you say," she replied, and she sent them away. After they had gone, she tied the scarlet cord to the window.

Notes

WHY DOES IT MATTER THAT WOMEN ARE INCLUDED IN THE GENEALOGY?

Matthew's genealogy explicitly includes the names of five women: Tamar, Rahab, Ruth, Uriah's wife, and Mary. It wasn't customary to include women in a Jewish genealogy, as the family line was traced through sons. Most scholars also believe that, other than Mary, the women included were not of Jewish descent. The inclusion of women in this genealogy reminds us that the promised Messiah was the hope for all nations and people, even those who were culturally marginalized.

[22] So the two men went into the hill country and stayed there three days until the pursuers had returned. They searched all along the way, but did not find them. [23] Then the men returned, came down from the hill country, and crossed the Jordan. They went to Joshua son of Nun and reported everything that had happened to them. [24] They told Joshua, "The Lord has handed over the entire land to us. Everyone who lives in the land is also panicking because of us."

FROM CHAPTER 6

Rahab and Her Family Spared

[22] Joshua said to the two men who had scouted the land, "Go to the prostitute's house and bring the woman out of there, and all who are with her, just as you swore to her."

[23] So the young men who had scouted went in and brought out Rahab and her father, mother, brothers, and all who belonged to her. They brought out her whole family and settled them outside the camp of Israel.

[24] They burned the city and everything in it, but they put the silver and gold and the articles of bronze and iron into the treasury of the Lord's house. [25] However, Joshua spared Rahab the prostitute, her father's family, and all who belonged to her, because she hid the messengers Joshua had sent to spy on Jericho, and she still lives in Israel today.

RESPONSE

01

What stood out to you
or surprised you about
Rahab's life?

02

From what you observed,
how would you describe Rahab's
relationship with God?

03

What did you relate to in
Rahab's story?

04

What connections did you see
in today's reading to the other
stories we've read?

RUTH AND BOAZ, A FAMILY LOST AND A FAMILY REDEEMED

Ruth was a Moabite widow who remained loyal to her mother-in-law, Naomi, by following Naomi to Israel after their husbands' deaths. Ruth was known for her faithfulness and hard work. **Boaz**, a relative of Noami's husband, married Ruth and provided a family for both women.

RUTH

FROM CHAPTER 1

Naomi's Family in Moab

¹ During the time of the judges, there was a famine in the land. A man left Bethlehem in Judah with his wife and two sons to stay in the territory of Moab for a while. ² The man's name was Elimelech, and his wife's name was Naomi. The names of his two sons were Mahlon and Chilion. They were Ephrathites from Bethlehem in Judah. They entered the fields of Moab and settled there. ³ Naomi's husband, Elimelech, died, and she was left with her two sons. ⁴ Her sons took Moabite women as their wives: one was named Orpah and the second was named Ruth. After they lived in Moab about ten years, ⁵ both Mahlon and Chilion also died, and

the woman was left without her two children and without her husband.

Ruth's Loyalty to Naomi

⁶ She and her daughters-in-law set out to return from the territory of Moab, because she had heard in Moab that the LORD had paid attention to his people's need by providing them food. ⁷ She left the place where she had been living, accompanied by her two daughters-in-law, and traveled along the road leading back to the land of Judah.

⁸ Naomi said to them, "Each of you go back to your mother's home. May the LORD show kindness to you as you have shown to the dead and to me. ⁹ May the LORD grant each of you rest in the house of a new husband." She kissed them, and they wept loudly.

¹⁰ They said to her, "We insist on returning with you to your people."

¹¹ But Naomi replied, "Return home, my daughters. Why do you want to go with me? Am I able to have any more sons who could become your husbands? ¹² Return home, my daughters. Go on, for I am too old to have another husband. Even if I thought there was still hope for me to have a husband tonight and to bear sons, ¹³ would you be willing to wait for them to grow up? Would you restrain yourselves from remarrying? No, my daughters, my life is much too bitter for you to share, because the LORD's hand has turned against me." ¹⁴ Again they wept loudly, and Orpah kissed her mother-in-law, but Ruth clung to her. ¹⁵ Naomi said, "Look, your sister-in-law has gone back to her people and to her gods. Follow your sister-in-law."

Notes

[16] But Ruth replied:

> Don't plead with me to abandon you
> or to return and not follow you.
> For wherever you go, I will go,
> and wherever you live, I will live;
> your people will be my people,
> and your God will be my God.
> [17] Where you die, I will die,
> and there I will be buried.
> May the LORD punish me,
> and do so severely,
> if anything but death separates you and me.

[18] When Naomi saw that Ruth was determined to go with her, she stopped talking to her.

FROM CHAPTER 2

Ruth and Boaz Meet

[1] Now Naomi had a relative on her husband's side. He was a prominent man of noble character from Elimelech's family. His name was Boaz.

[2] Ruth the Moabitess asked Naomi, "Will you let me go into the fields and gather fallen grain behind someone with whom I find favor?"

Naomi answered her, "Go ahead, my daughter." [3] So Ruth left and entered the field to gather grain behind the harvesters. She happened to be in the portion of the field belonging to Boaz, who was from Elimelech's family.

…

[19] Her mother-in-law said to her, "Where did you gather barley today, and where did you work? May the LORD bless the man who noticed you."

Ruth told her mother-in-law whom she had worked with and said, "The name of the man I worked with today is Boaz."

[20] Then Naomi said to her daughter-in-law, "May the LORD bless him because he has not abandoned his kindness to the living or the dead." Naomi continued, "The man is a close relative. He is one of our family redeemers."

[21] Ruth the Moabitess said, "He also told me, 'Stay with my young men until they have finished all of my harvest.'"

²² So Naomi said to her daughter-in-law Ruth, "My daughter, it is good for you to work with his female servants, so that nothing will happen to you in another field." ²³ Ruth stayed close to Boaz's female servants and gathered grain until the barley and the wheat harvests were finished. And she lived with her mother-in-law.

FROM CHAPTER 3

Ruth's Appeal to Boaz

¹ Ruth's mother-in-law Naomi said to her, "My daughter, shouldn't I find rest for you, so that you will be taken care of? ² Now isn't Boaz our relative? Haven't you been working with his female servants? This evening he will be winnowing barley on the threshing floor. ³ Wash, put on perfumed oil, and wear your best clothes. Go down to the threshing floor, but don't let the man know you are there until he has finished eating and drinking. ⁴ When he lies down, notice the place where he's lying, go in and uncover his feet, and lie down. Then he will explain to you what you should do."

⁵ So Ruth said to her, "I will do everything you say." ⁶ She went down to the threshing floor and did everything her mother-in-law had charged her to do. ⁷ After Boaz ate, drank, and was in good spirits, he went to lie down at the end of the pile of barley, and she came secretly, uncovered his feet, and lay down.

⁸ At midnight, Boaz was startled, turned over, and there lying at his feet was a woman! ⁹ So he asked, "Who are you?"

"I am Ruth, your servant," she replied.

"Take me under your wing, for you are a family redeemer."

¹⁰ Then he said, "May the LORD bless you, my daughter. You have shown more kindness now than before, because you have not pursued younger men, whether rich or poor. ¹¹ Now don't be afraid, my daughter. I will do for you whatever you say, since all the people in my town know that you are a woman of noble character. ¹² Yes, it is true that I am a family redeemer, but there is a redeemer closer than I am. ¹³ Stay here tonight, and in the morning, if he wants to redeem you, that's good. Let him redeem you. But if he doesn't want to redeem you, as the LORD lives, I will. Now lie down until morning."

FROM CHAPTER 4

Ruth and Boaz Marry

¹ Boaz went to the gate of the town and sat down there. Soon the family redeemer Boaz had spoken about came by. Boaz said, "Come over here and sit down." So he went over and sat down. ² Then Boaz took ten men of the town's elders and said,

Notes

"Sit here." And they sat down. ³ He said to the redeemer, "Naomi, who has returned from the territory of Moab, is selling the portion of the field that belonged to our brother Elimelech. ⁴ I thought I should inform you: Buy it back in the presence of those seated here and in the presence of the elders of my people. If you want to redeem it, do it. But if you do not want to redeem it, tell me so that I will know, because there isn't anyone other than you to redeem it, and I am next after you."

"I want to redeem it," he answered.

⁵ Then Boaz said, "On the day you buy the field from Naomi, you will acquire Ruth the Moabitess, the wife of the deceased man, to perpetuate the man's name on his property."

⁶ The redeemer replied, "I can't redeem it myself, or I will ruin my own inheritance. Take my right of redemption, because I can't redeem it."

⁷ At an earlier period in Israel, a man removed his sandal and gave it to the other party in order to make any matter legally binding concerning the right of redemption or the exchange of property. This was the method of legally binding a transaction in Israel.

⁸ So the redeemer removed his sandal and said to Boaz, "Buy back the property yourself."

⁹ Boaz said to the elders and all the people, "You are witnesses today that I am buying from Naomi everything that belonged to Elimelech, Chilion, and Mahlon. ¹⁰ I have also acquired Ruth the Moabitess, Mahlon's widow, as my wife, to perpetuate the deceased man's name on his property, so that his name will not disappear among his relatives or from the gate of his hometown. You are witnesses today."

¹¹ All the people who were at the city gate, including the elders, said, "We are witnesses. May the Lord make the woman who is entering your house like Rachel and Leah, who together built the house of Israel. May you be powerful in Ephrathah and your name well known in Bethlehem. ¹² May your house become like the house of Perez, the son Tamar bore to Judah, because of the offspring the Lord will give you by this young woman."

¹³ Boaz took Ruth and she became his wife. He slept with her, and the Lord granted conception to her, and she gave birth to a son. ¹⁴ The women said to Naomi, "Blessed be the Lord, who has not left you without a family redeemer today. May his name become well known in Israel. ¹⁵ He will renew your life and sustain you in your old age. Indeed, your daughter-in-law, who loves you and is better to you than seven sons, has given birth to him." ¹⁶ Naomi took the child, placed him on her lap, and became a mother to him.

RESPONSE

01

What stood out to you or surprised you about Ruth's and Boaz's lives?

02

From what you observed, how would you describe Ruth's and Boaz's relationships with God?

03

What did you relate to in Ruth and Boaz's story/stories?

04

What connections did you see in today's reading to the other stories we've read?

THE SON OF...

SON OF GOD

In the Old Testament, "sons of God" referred to those who were specially appointed to carry out God's will, like kings or heavenly beings. In the New Testament, this language is used for Jesus, God the Son. The title is a reminder that He is the divine King who has the right and authority to carry out God's purposes.

MT 14:33; 27:40; MK 1:1; 3:11; JN 1:34

SON OF MAN

In the book of Daniel, the young Israelite sees a vision of the "son of man," one like a human being, appearing before the throne of the Ancient of Days (Dn 7:9–14). More than just an ordinary human, he is a figure of hope and triumph—exalted and not defeated—who reigns with God. In the Gospels, Jesus repeatedly refers to Himself as the Son of Man, confirming Himself as the answer to Daniel's vision.

MT 8:20; LK 12:8; 22:69; JN 6:27

SON OF DAVID

David was the second king over Israel, chosen by God as a young shepherd boy to faithfully lead His people. Though David was an imperfect person and leader, he was still a man after God's heart. When God called David to be king, He promised that, through David's house, He would establish a kingdom that would never end (2Sm 7:12–16). Even after the kingdom of Israel divided, and generations of mostly unfaithful kings followed, God never forgot His promise. Jesus is the promised true King and Messiah for Israel.

MT 1:1; 9:27; MK 12:35

THROUGHOUT THE NEW TESTAMENT, JESUS IS REFERENCED AS "THE SON OF" SEVERAL DIFFERENT ENTITIES. SOME OF THESE TITLES EMPHASIZE HIS IDENTITY, OTHERS DEMONSTRATE WHAT HE CAME TO FULFILL AND ACCOMPLISH. INCLUDED HERE ARE THE NAMES OF SONSHIP ATTRIBUTED TO JESUS ALONG WITH AN EXPLANATION.

SON OF ABRAHAM

God called Abraham to leave his home and follow God to a new land. God promised to make Abraham into a great nation, and through his descendents, God would bless every nation on earth (Gn 12:1–9; 15; 17:1–8). God would use the people of Israel to fulfill that promise and Jesus would ultimately be the source of eternal blessing to the whole world.

MT 1:1

SON OF MARY

In the garden of Eden, after Adam and Eve had sinned, God declared that there would be hostility between the offspring of the serpent and the woman (Gn 3:15). Jesus is the ultimate descendent of Eve, born of another woman, Mary. He would strike the enemy down once and for all through His death, resurrection, ascension, and return.

MK 6:3

SON OF JOSEPH

Jesus was raised by His earthly father, Joseph. It is through Joseph's family line that we trace Jesus's ancestry, situating Him in the human lineage of both Adam and Abraham.

LK 4:22; JN 1:45

DAVID, ANOINTED SHEPHERD

After Saul, the first king of Israel, disobeyed God, the prophet Samuel sought out Jesse to anoint one of his sons as the future king. **David** was the youngest son of Jesse. He succeeded Saul as the second king of Israel. During his life and reign, David disobeyed God on several occasions. But because of his posture of repentance before God, he was called a man after God's heart.

---

1 SAMUEL

FROM CHAPTER 15

¹⁶ "Stop!" exclaimed Samuel. "Let me tell you what the LORD said to me last night."

"Tell me," he replied.

¹⁷ Samuel continued, "Although you once considered yourself unimportant, haven't you become the leader of the tribes of Israel? The LORD anointed you king over Israel ¹⁸ and then sent you on a mission and said, 'Go and completely destroy the sinful Amalekites. Fight against them until you have annihilated them.' ¹⁹ So why didn't you obey the LORD? Why did you rush on the plunder and do what was evil in the LORD's sight?"

²⁰ "But I did obey the LORD!" Saul answered. "I went on the mission the LORD gave me: I brought back King Agag of Amalek, and I completely destroyed the Amalekites. ²¹ The troops took sheep, goats, and cattle from the plunder—the best of what was set apart for destruction—to sacrifice to the LORD your God at Gilgal."

²² Then Samuel said:

> Does the LORD take pleasure in burnt offerings and sacrifices
> as much as in obeying the LORD?
> Look: to obey is better than sacrifice,
> to pay attention is better than the fat of rams.
> ²³ For rebellion is like the sin of divination,
> and defiance is like wickedness and idolatry.
> Because you have rejected the word of the LORD,
> he has rejected you as king.

1 CHRONICLES

FROM CHAPTER 2

[11] Nahshon fathered Salma, and Salma fathered Boaz. [12] Boaz fathered Obed, and Obed fathered Jesse. [13] Jesse fathered Eliab, his firstborn; Abinadab was born second, Shimea third, [14] Nethanel fourth, Raddai fifth, [15] Ozem sixth, and David seventh.

1 SAMUEL

FROM CHAPTER 16

Samuel Anoints David

[1] The LORD said to Samuel, "How long are you going to mourn for Saul, since I have rejected him as king over Israel? Fill your horn with oil and go. I am sending you to Jesse of Bethlehem because I have selected for myself a king from his sons."

[2] Samuel asked, "How can I go? Saul will hear about it and kill me!"

The LORD answered, "Take a young cow with you and say, 'I have come to sacrifice to the LORD.' [3] Then invite Jesse to the sacrifice, and I will let you know what you are to do. You are to anoint for me the one I indicate to you."

[4] Samuel did what the LORD directed and went to Bethlehem. When the elders of the town met him, they trembled and asked, "Do you come in peace?"

[5] "In peace," he replied. "I've come to sacrifice to the LORD. Consecrate yourselves and come with me to the sacrifice." Then he consecrated Jesse and his sons and invited them to the sacrifice. [6] When they arrived, Samuel saw Eliab and said, "Certainly the LORD's anointed one is here before him."

[7] But the LORD said to Samuel, "Do not look at his appearance or his stature because I have rejected him. Humans do not see what the LORD sees, for humans see what is visible, but the LORD sees the heart."

[8] Jesse called Abinadab and presented him to Samuel. "The LORD hasn't chosen this one either," Samuel said. [9] Then Jesse presented Shammah, but Samuel said, "The LORD hasn't chosen this one either." [10] After Jesse presented seven of his sons to him, Samuel told Jesse, "The LORD hasn't chosen any of these." [11] Samuel asked him, "Are these all the sons you have?"

"There is still the youngest," he answered, "but right now he's tending the sheep." Samuel told Jesse, "Send for him. We won't sit down to eat until he gets here." [12] So Jesse sent for him. He had beautiful eyes and a healthy, handsome appearance.

Then the LORD said, "Anoint him, for he is the one." [13] So Samuel took the horn of oil and anointed him in the presence of his brothers, and the Spirit of the LORD came powerfully on David from that day forward. Then Samuel set out and went to Ramah.

2 SAMUEL

FROM CHAPTER 5

[4] David was thirty years old when he began his reign; he reigned forty years.

…

[9] David took up residence in the stronghold, which he named the city of David. He built it up all the way around from the supporting terraces inward. [10] David became more and more powerful, and the LORD God of Armies was with him. [11] King Hiram of Tyre sent envoys to David; he also sent cedar logs, carpenters, and stonemasons, and they built a palace for David. [12] Then David knew that the LORD had established him as king over Israel and had exalted his kingdom for the sake of his people Israel.

FROM CHAPTER 7

The Lord's Covenant with David

[1] When the king had settled into his palace and the LORD had given him rest on every side from all his enemies, [2] the king said to the prophet Nathan, "Look, I am living in a cedar house while the ark of God sits inside tent curtains."

[3] So Nathan told the king, "Go and do all that is on your mind, for the LORD is with you."

4 But that night the word of the LORD came to Nathan: 5 "Go to my servant David and say, 'This is what the LORD says: Are you to build me a house to dwell in? 6 From the time I brought the Israelites out of Egypt until today I have not dwelt in a house; instead, I have been moving around with a tent as my dwelling. 7 In all my journeys with all the Israelites, have I ever spoken a word to one of the tribal leaders of Israel, whom I commanded to shepherd my people Israel, asking: Why haven't you built me a house of cedar?'

8 "So now this is what you are to say to my servant David: 'This is what the LORD of Armies says: I took you from the pasture, from tending the flock, to be ruler over my people Israel. 9 I have been with you wherever you have gone, and I have destroyed all your enemies before you. I will make a great name for you like that of the greatest on the earth. 10 I will designate a place for my people Israel and plant them, so that they may live there and not be disturbed again. Evildoers will not continue to oppress them as they have done 11 ever since the day I ordered judges to be over my people Israel. I will give you rest from all your enemies.

"'The LORD declares to you: The LORD himself will make a house for you. 12 When your time comes and you rest with your ancestors, I will raise up after you your descendant, who will come from your body, and I will establish his kingdom. 13 He is the one who will build a house for my name, and I will establish the throne of his kingdom forever. 14 I will be his father, and he will be my son. When he does wrong, I will discipline him with a rod of men and blows from mortals. 15 But my faithful love will never leave him as it did when I removed it from Saul, whom I removed from before you. 16 Your house and kingdom will endure before me forever, and your throne will be established forever.'"

17 Nathan reported all these words and this entire vision to David.

David's Prayer of Thanksgiving

18 Then King David went in, sat in the LORD's presence, and said,

> Who am I, Lord GOD, and what is my house that you have brought me this far?

19 What you have done so far was a little thing to you, Lord GOD, for you have also spoken about your servant's house in the distant future. And this is a revelation for mankind, Lord GOD. 20 What more can David say to you? You know your servant, Lord GOD. 21 Because of your word and according to your will, you have revealed all these great things to your servant.

22 This is why you are great, Lord GOD. There is no one like you, and there is no God besides you, as all we have heard confirms. 23 And who is like your people Israel? God came to one nation on earth in order to redeem a people for himself, to make a name for himself, and to perform for them great and awesome acts, driving out nations and their gods before your people you redeemed for yourself from Egypt. 24 You established your people Israel to be your own people forever, and you, LORD, have become their God.

PSALMS

FROM CHAPTER 51

A Prayer for Restoration

For the choir director. A psalm of David, when the prophet Nathan came to him after he had gone to Bathsheba.

1 Be gracious to me, God,
according to your faithful love;
according to your abundant compassion,
blot out my rebellion.
2 Completely wash away my guilt
and cleanse me from my sin.
3 For I am conscious of my rebellion,
and my sin is always before me.
4 Against you—you alone—I have sinned
and done this evil in your sight.
So you are right when you pass sentence;
you are blameless when you judge.
5 Indeed, I was guilty when I was born;
I was sinful when my mother conceived me.

6 Surely you desire integrity in the inner self,
and you teach me wisdom deep within.
7 Purify me with hyssop, and I will be clean;
wash me, and I will be whiter than snow.
8 Let me hear joy and gladness;
let the bones you have crushed rejoice.
9 Turn your face away from my sins
and blot out all my guilt.

01

What stood out to you or
surprised you about David's life?

02

From what you observed,
how would you describe David's
relationship with God?

03

What did you relate to in
David's story?

04

What connections did you see
in today's reading to the other
stories we've read?

BATHSHEBA, URIAH'S WIFE

Uriah's wife refers to Bathsheba, a Hittite woman who was the wife of one of King David's most trusted warriors. After King David committed sexual sin against Bathsheba and she became pregnant, David had her husband Uriah killed in an attempt to cover up his own actions. Bathsheba became one of David's wives and gave birth to Solomon. She later persuaded David to make Solomon king, even though Solomon was not the oldest son.

2 SAMUEL

FROM CHAPTER 11

David's Adultery with Bathsheba

[1] In the spring when kings march out to war, David sent Joab with his officers and all Israel. They destroyed the Ammonites and besieged Rabbah, but David remained in Jerusalem.

[2] One evening David got up from his bed and strolled around on the roof of the palace. From the roof he saw a woman bathing—a very beautiful woman. [3] So David sent someone to inquire about her, and he said, "Isn't this Bathsheba, daughter of Eliam and wife of Uriah the Hethite?"

[4] David sent messengers to get her, and when she came to him, he slept with her. Now she had just been purifying

herself from her uncleanness. Afterward, she returned home. [5] The woman conceived and sent word to inform David, "I am pregnant."

[6] David sent orders to Joab: "Send me Uriah the Hethite." So Joab sent Uriah to David. [7] When Uriah came to him, David asked how Joab and the troops were doing and how the war was going. [8] Then he said to Uriah, "Go down to your house and wash your feet." So Uriah left the palace, and a gift from the king followed him. [9] But Uriah slept at the door of the palace with all his master's servants; he did not go down to his house.

[10] When it was reported to David, "Uriah didn't go home," David questioned Uriah, "Haven't you just come from a journey? Why didn't you go home?"

[11] Uriah answered David, "The ark, Israel, and Judah are dwelling in tents, and my master Joab and his soldiers are camping in the open field. How can I enter my house to eat and drink and sleep with my wife? As surely as you live and by your life, I will not do this!"

[12] "Stay here today also," David said to Uriah, "and tomorrow I will send you back." So Uriah stayed in Jerusalem that day and the next. [13] Then David invited Uriah to eat and drink with him, and David got him drunk. He went out in the evening to lie down on his cot with his master's servants, but he did not go home.

Uriah's Death Arranged

[14] The next morning David wrote a letter to Joab and sent it with Uriah. [15] In the letter he wrote:

> Put Uriah at the front of the fiercest fighting, then withdraw from him so that he is struck down and dies.

[16] When Joab was besieging the city, he put Uriah in the place where he knew the best enemy soldiers were. [17] Then the men of the city came out and attacked Joab, and some of the men from David's soldiers fell in battle; Uriah the Hethite also died.

…

[26] When Uriah's wife heard that her husband, Uriah, had died, she mourned for him. [27] When the time of mourning ended, David had her brought to his house.

She became his wife and bore him a son.

However, the LORD considered what David had done to be evil.

Notes

Notes

Nathan's Parable and David's Repentance

[1] So the LORD sent Nathan to David. When he arrived, he said to him:

There were two men in a certain city, one rich and the other poor. [2] The rich man had very large flocks and herds, [3] but the poor man had nothing except one small ewe lamb that he had bought. He raised her, and she grew up with him and with his children. From his meager food she would eat, from his cup she would drink, and in his arms she would sleep. She was like a daughter to him. [4] Now a traveler came to the rich man, but the rich man could not bring himself to take one of his own sheep or cattle to prepare for the traveler who had come to him. Instead, he took the poor man's lamb and prepared it for his guest.

[5] David was infuriated with the man and said to Nathan, "As the LORD lives, the man who did this deserves to die! [6] Because he has done this thing and shown no pity, he must pay four lambs for that lamb."

[7] Nathan replied to David, "You are the man! This is what the LORD God of Israel says: 'I anointed you king over Israel, and I rescued you from Saul. [8] I gave your master's house to you and your master's wives into your arms, and I gave you the house of Israel and Judah, and if that was not enough, I would have given you even more. [9] Why then have you despised the LORD's command by doing what I consider evil? You struck down Uriah the Hethite with the sword and took his wife as your own wife—you murdered him with the Ammonite's sword. [10] Now therefore, the sword will never leave your house because you despised me and took the wife of Uriah the Hethite to be your own wife.'

[11] "This is what the LORD says, 'I am going to bring disaster on you from your own family: I will take your wives and give them to another before your very eyes, and he will sleep with them in broad daylight. [12] You acted in secret, but I will do this before all Israel and in broad daylight.'"

[13] David responded to Nathan, "I have sinned against the LORD."

Then Nathan replied to David, "And the LORD has taken away your sin; you will not die. [14] However, because you treated the LORD with such contempt in this matter, the son born to you will die." [15] Then Nathan went home.

The Death of Bathsheba's Son

The LORD struck the baby that Uriah's wife had borne to David, and he became deathly ill. [16] David pleaded with God for the boy. He fasted, went home, and spent the night lying on the ground. [17] The elders of his house stood beside him to get him up from the ground, but he was unwilling and would not eat anything with them.

[18] On the seventh day the baby died. But David's servants were afraid to tell him the baby was dead. They said, "Look, while the baby was alive, we spoke to him, and he wouldn't listen to us. So how can we tell him the baby is dead? He may do something desperate."

[19] When David saw that his servants were whispering to each other, he guessed that the baby was dead. So he asked his servants, "Is the baby dead?"

"He is dead," they replied.

[20] Then David got up from the ground. He washed, anointed himself, changed his clothes, went to the LORD's house, and worshiped. Then he went home and requested something to eat. So they served him food, and he ate.

[21] His servants asked him, "Why have you done this? While the baby was alive, you fasted and wept, but when he died, you got up and ate food."

[22] He answered, "While the baby was alive, I fasted and wept because I thought, 'Who knows? The LORD may be gracious to me and let him live.' [23] But now that he is dead, why should I fast? Can I bring him back again? I'll go to him, but he will never return to me."

The Birth of Solomon

[24] Then David comforted his wife Bathsheba; he went to her and slept with her. She gave birth to a son and named him Solomon. The LORD loved him, [25] and he sent a message through the prophet Nathan, who named him Jedidiah, because of the LORD.

1 KINGS

FROM CHAPTER 1

Nathan's and Bathsheba's Appeals

[11] Then Nathan said to Bathsheba, Solomon's mother, "Have you not heard that Adonijah son of Haggith has become king and our lord David does not know it? [12] Now please come and let me advise you. Save your life and the life of your son Solomon. [13] Go, approach King David and say to him, 'My lord the king, did you not swear to your servant: Your son Solomon is to become king after me, and he is the one who is to sit on my throne? So why has Adonijah become king?' [14] At that

Notes

moment, while you are still there speaking with the king, I'll come in after you and confirm your words."

[15] So Bathsheba went to the king in his bedroom. Since the king was very old, Abishag the Shunammite was attending to him. [16] Bathsheba knelt low and paid homage to the king, and he asked, "What do you want?"

[17] She replied, "My lord, you swore to your servant by the LORD your God, 'Your son Solomon is to become king after me, and he is the one who is to sit on my throne.' [18] Now look, Adonijah has become king. And, my lord the king, you didn't know it. [19] He has lavishly sacrificed oxen, fattened cattle, and sheep. He invited all the king's sons, the priest Abiathar, and Joab the commander of the army, but he did not invite your servant Solomon. [20] Now, my lord the king, the eyes of all Israel are on you to tell them who will sit on the throne of my lord the king after him. [21] Otherwise, when my lord the king rests with his ancestors, I and my son Solomon will be regarded as criminals."

[22] At that moment, while she was still speaking with the king, the prophet Nathan arrived, [23] and it was announced to the king, "The prophet Nathan is here." He came into the king's presence and paid homage to him with his face to the ground.

[24] "My lord the king," Nathan said, "did you say, 'Adonijah is to become king after me, and he is the one who is to sit on my throne'? [25] For today he went down and lavishly sacrificed oxen, fattened cattle, and sheep. He invited all the sons of the king, the commanders of the army, and the priest Abiathar. And look! They're eating and drinking in his presence, and they're saying, 'Long live King Adonijah!' [26] But he did not invite me—me, your servant—or the priest Zadok or Benaiah son of Jehoiada or your servant Solomon. [27] I'm certain my lord the king would not have let this happen without letting your servant know who will sit on my lord the king's throne after him."

Solomon Confirmed King

[28] King David responded by saying, "Call in Bathsheba for me." So she came into the king's presence and stood before him. [29] The king swore an oath and said, "As the LORD lives, who has redeemed my life from every difficulty, [30] just as I swore to you by the LORD God of Israel: Your son Solomon is to become king after me, and he is the one who is to sit on my throne in my place, that is exactly what I will do this very day."

[31] Bathsheba knelt low with her face to the ground, paying homage to the king, and said, "May my lord King David live forever!"

RESPONSE

01

What stood out to you
or surprised you about
Bathsheba's life?

02

From what you observed, how
would you describe Bathsheba's
relationship with God?

03

What did you relate to in
Bathsheba's story?

04

What connections did you see
in today's reading to the other
stories we've read?

GRACE DAY

Take this day to catch up on your reading, pray, and rest in the presence of the Lord.

KNOW THAT THE LORD YOUR GOD IS GOD, THE FAITHFUL GOD WHO KEEPS HIS GRACIOUS COVENANT LOYALTY FOR A THOUSAND GENERATIONS WITH THOSE WHO LOVE HIM AND KEEP HIS COMMANDS.

DEUTERONOMY 7:9

WEEKLY

Day 21

TRUTH

THE GENEALOGY OF JESUS

Scripture is God-breathed and true. When we memorize it,
we carry the good news of Jesus with us wherever we go.

As we continue to memorize Romans 8:14–17, we'll add verse 16,
which points us to the Spirit who echoes that believers are indeed
God's children.

^{14} FOR ALL THOSE LED BY GOD'S SPIRIT ARE
GOD'S SONS. ^{15} FOR YOU DID NOT RECEIVE
A SPIRIT OF SLAVERY TO FALL BACK INTO
FEAR. INSTEAD, YOU RECEIVED THE SPIRIT OF
ADOPTION, BY WHOM WE CRY OUT, "*ABBA,
FATHER!*" ^{16} THE SPIRIT HIMSELF TESTIFIES
TOGETHER WITH OUR SPIRIT THAT WE ARE
GOD'S CHILDREN, ^{17} AND IF CHILDREN, ALSO
HEIRS—HEIRS OF GOD AND COHEIRS WITH
CHRIST—IF INDEED WE SUFFER WITH HIM SO
THAT WE MAY ALSO BE GLORIFIED WITH HIM.

ROMANS 8:14–17

See tips for memorizing Scripture on page 172.

Day 22

SOLOMON, WHO ASKED FOR WISDOM

Solomon was the last king to reign over the united nation of Israel. Early in his reign, he asked God for wisdom. He later led the construction of the first temple. Yet he compromised his faithfulness to God by marrying hundreds of women who did not worship God, personally committing idolatry, and oppressing the people.

1 KINGS

FROM CHAPTER 1

³² King David then said, "Call in the priest Zadok, the prophet Nathan, and Benaiah son of Jehoiada for me." So they came into the king's presence. ³³ The king said to them, "Take my servants with you, have my son Solomon ride on my own mule, and take him down to Gihon. ³⁴ There, the priest Zadok and the prophet Nathan are to anoint him as king over Israel. You are to blow the ram's horn and say, 'Long live King Solomon!' ³⁵ You are to come up after him, and he is to come in and sit on my throne. He is the one who is to become king in my place; he is the one I have commanded to be ruler over Israel and Judah."

³⁶ "Amen," Benaiah son of Jehoiada replied to the king. "May the Lᴏʀᴅ, the God of my lord the king, so affirm it. ³⁷ Just as the Lᴏʀᴅ was with my lord the king, so may he be with Solomon and make his throne greater than the throne of my lord King David."

³⁸ Then the priest Zadok, the prophet Nathan, Benaiah son of Jehoiada, the Cherethites, and the Pelethites went down, had Solomon ride on King David's mule, and took him to Gihon. ³⁹ The priest Zadok took the horn of oil from the tabernacle and anointed Solomon. Then they blew the ram's horn, and all the people proclaimed, "Long live King Solomon!" ⁴⁰ All the people went up after him, playing flutes and rejoicing with such a great joy that the earth split open from the sound.

FROM CHAPTER 3

The Lord Appears to Solomon

¹ Solomon made an alliance with Pharaoh king of Egypt by marrying Pharaoh's daughter. Solomon brought her to the city of David until he finished building his palace, the Lᴏʀᴅ's temple, and the wall surrounding Jerusalem. ² However, the

112 THE GENEALOGY OF JESUS

people were sacrificing on the high places, because until that time a temple for the LORD's name had not been built. ³ Solomon loved the LORD by walking in the statutes of his father David, but he also sacrificed and burned incense on the high places.

⁴ The king went to Gibeon to sacrifice there because it was the most famous high place. He offered a thousand burnt offerings on that altar. ⁵ At Gibeon the LORD appeared to Solomon in a dream at night. God said, "Ask. What should I give you?"

⁶ And Solomon replied, "You have shown great and faithful love to your servant, my father David, because he walked before you in faithfulness, righteousness, and integrity. You have continued this great and faithful love for him by giving him a son to sit on his throne, as it is today.

⁷ "LORD my God, you have now made your servant king in my father David's place. Yet I am just a youth with no experience in leadership. ⁸ Your servant is among your people you have chosen, a people too many to be numbered or counted. ⁹ So give your servant a receptive heart to judge your people and to discern between good and evil. For who is able to judge this great people of yours?"

¹⁰ Now it pleased the Lord that Solomon had requested this. ¹¹ So God said to him, "Because you have requested this and did not ask for long life or riches for yourself, or the death of your enemies, but you asked discernment for yourself to administer justice, ¹² I will therefore do what you have asked. I will give you a wise and understanding heart, so that there has never been anyone like you before and never will be again. ¹³ In addition, I will give you what you did not ask for: both riches and honor, so that no king will be your equal during your entire life. ¹⁴ If you walk in my ways and keep my statutes and commands just as your father David did, I will give you a long life."

¹⁵ Then Solomon woke up and realized it had been a dream. He went to Jerusalem, stood before the ark of the Lord's covenant, and offered burnt offerings and fellowship offerings. Then he held a feast for all his servants.

FROM CHAPTER 4

Solomon's Wisdom and Literary Gifts

²⁹ God gave Solomon wisdom, very great insight, and understanding as vast as the sand on the seashore. ³⁰ Solomon's wisdom was greater than the wisdom of all the people of the East, greater than all the wisdom of Egypt. ³¹ He was wiser than anyone—wiser than Ethan the Ezrahite, and Heman, Calcol, and Darda, sons of Mahol. His reputation extended to all the surrounding nations.

Notes

Notes

FROM CHAPTER 8

[35] When the skies are shut and there is no rain,
because they have sinned against you,
and they pray toward this place
and praise your name,
and they turn from their sins
because you are afflicting them,
[36] may you hear in heaven
and forgive the sin of your servants
and your people Israel,
so that you may teach them to walk on the good way.
May you send rain on your land
that you gave your people for an inheritance.
[37] When there is famine in the land,
when there is pestilence,
when there is blight or mildew, locust or grasshopper,
when their enemy besieges them
in the land and its cities,
when there is any plague or illness,
[38] every prayer or petition
that any person or that all your people Israel may have—
they each know their own affliction—
as they spread out their hands toward this temple,
[39] may you hear in heaven, your dwelling place,
and may you forgive, act, and give to everyone
according to all their ways, since you know each heart,
for you alone know every human heart,
[40] so that they may fear you
all the days they live on the land
you gave our ancestors.

…

[51] For they are your people and your inheritance;
you brought them out of Egypt,
out of the middle of an iron furnace.
[52] May your eyes be open to your servant's petition
and to the petition of your people Israel,
listening to them whenever they call to you.
[53] For you, Lord GOD, have set them apart as your inheritance
from all peoples of the earth,
as you spoke through your servant Moses
when you brought our ancestors out of Egypt.

Solomon's Blessing

54 When Solomon finished praying this entire prayer and petition to the LORD, he got up from kneeling before the altar of the LORD, with his hands spread out toward heaven, 55 and he stood and blessed the whole congregation of Israel with a loud voice: 56 "Blessed be the LORD! He has given rest to his people Israel according to all he has said. Not one of all the good promises he made through his servant Moses has failed. 57 May the LORD our God be with us as he was with our ancestors. May he not abandon us or leave us 58 so that he causes us to be devoted to him, to walk in all his ways, and to keep his commands, statutes, and ordinances, which he commanded our ancestors. 59 May my words with which I have made my petition before the LORD be near the LORD our God day and night. May he uphold his servant's cause and the cause of his people Israel, as each day requires. 60 May all the peoples of the earth know that the LORD is God. There is no other! 61 Be wholeheartedly devoted to the LORD our God to walk in his statutes and to keep his commands, as it is today."

FROM CHAPTER 9

The Lord's Response

1 When Solomon finished building the temple of the LORD, the royal palace, and all that Solomon desired to do, 2 the LORD appeared to Solomon a second time just as he had appeared to him at Gibeon. 3 The LORD said to him:

I have heard your prayer and petition you have made before me. I have consecrated this temple you have built, to put my name there forever; my eyes and my heart will be there at all times.

4 As for you, if you walk before me as your father David walked, with a heart of integrity and in what is right, doing everything I have commanded you, and if you keep my statutes and ordinances, 5 I will establish your royal throne over Israel forever, as I promised your father David: You will never fail to have a man on the throne of Israel.

6 If you or your sons turn away from following me and do not keep my commands—my statutes that I have set before you—and if you go and serve other gods and bow in worship to them, 7 I will cut off Israel from the land I gave them, and I will reject the temple I have sanctified for my name. Israel will become an object of scorn and ridicule among all the peoples.

FROM CHAPTER 11

Solomon's Unfaithfulness to God

1 King Solomon loved many foreign women in addition to Pharaoh's daughter: Moabite, Ammonite, Edomite, Sidonian, and Hittite women 2 from the nations about which the LORD had told the Israelites, "You must not intermarry with

Notes

them, and they must not intermarry with you, because they will turn your heart away to follow their gods." To these women Solomon was deeply attached in love. [3] He had seven hundred wives who were princesses and three hundred who were concubines, and they turned his heart away.

[4] When Solomon was old, his wives turned his heart away to follow other gods. He was not wholeheartedly devoted to the LORD his God, as his father David had been.

…

[9] The LORD was angry with Solomon, because his heart had turned away from the LORD, the God of Israel, who had appeared to him twice. [10] He had commanded him about this, so that he would not follow other gods, but Solomon did not do what the LORD had commanded.

[11] Then the LORD said to Solomon, "Since you have done this and did not keep my covenant and my statutes, which I commanded you, I will tear the kingdom away from you and give it to your servant. [12] However, I will not do it during your lifetime for the sake of your father David; I will tear it out of your son's hand. [13] Yet I will not tear the entire kingdom away from him. I will give one tribe to your son for the sake of my servant David and for the sake of Jerusalem that I chose."

…

[26] Now Solomon's servant, Jeroboam son of Nebat, was an Ephraimite from Zeredah. His widowed mother's name was Zeruah. Jeroboam rebelled against Solomon, [27] and this is the reason he rebelled against the king: Solomon had built the supporting terraces and repaired the opening in the wall of the city of his father David. [28] Now the man Jeroboam was capable, and Solomon noticed the young man because he was getting things done. So he appointed him over the entire labor force of the house of Joseph.

[29] During that time, the prophet Ahijah the Shilonite met Jeroboam on the road as Jeroboam came out of Jerusalem. Now Ahijah had wrapped himself with a new cloak, and the two of them were alone in the open field. [30] Then Ahijah took hold of the new cloak he had on, tore it into twelve pieces, [31] and said to Jeroboam, "Take ten pieces for yourself, for this is what the LORD God of Israel says: 'I am about to tear the kingdom out of Solomon's hand. I will give you ten tribes, [32] but one tribe will remain his for the sake of my servant David and for the sake of Jerusalem, the city I chose out of all the tribes of Israel. [33] For they have abandoned me; they have bowed down to Ashtoreth, the goddess of the Sidonians, to Chemosh, the god of Moab, and to Milcom, the god of the Ammonites. They have not walked in my ways to do what is right in my sight and to carry out my statutes and my judgments as his father David did.

[34] "'However, I will not take the whole kingdom from him but will let him be ruler all the days of his life for the sake of my servant David, whom I chose and who kept my commands and my statutes. [35] I will take ten tribes of the kingdom from his son and give them to you. [36] I will give one tribe to his son, so that my servant David will always have a lamp before me in Jerusalem, the city I chose for myself to put my name there. [37] I will appoint you, and you will reign as king over all you want, and you will be king over Israel.

[38] "'After that, if you obey all I command you, walk in my ways, and do what is right in my sight in order to keep my statutes and my commands as my servant David did, I will be with you. I will build you a lasting dynasty just as I built for David, and I will give you Israel. [39] I will humble David's descendants, because of their unfaithfulness, but not forever.'"

[40] Therefore, Solomon tried to kill Jeroboam, but he fled to Egypt, to King Shishak of Egypt, where he remained until Solomon's death.

Solomon's Death

[41] The rest of the events of Solomon's reign, along with all his accomplishments and his wisdom, are written in the Book of Solomon's Events. [42] The length of Solomon's reign in Jerusalem over all Israel totaled forty years. [43] Solomon rested with his ancestors and was buried in the city of his father David. His son Rehoboam became king in his place.

RESPONSE

01

What stood out to you
or surprised you about
Solomon's life?

02

From what you observed,
how would you describe
Solomon's relationship with God?

03

What did you relate to in
Solomon's story?

04

What connections did you see
in today's reading to the other
stories we've read?

REHOBOAM, WHO BURDENED GOD'S PEOPLE

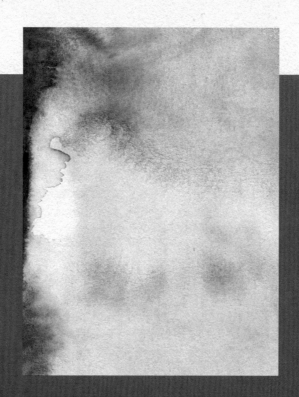

Rehoboam was the first king of the southern kingdom
of Judah after a civil war divided the nation. He imposed
unbearable labor demands on Israel, leading all of the tribes
except Judah and Benjamin to reject him as king. Rehoboam
ultimately rejected God and led the people to the same end,
calling them to worship other gods, including two golden
calves—the same symbol the people of Israel worshiped
after they escaped from Egypt.

2 CHRONICLES

FROM CHAPTER 10

The Kingdom Divided

¹ Then Rehoboam went to Shechem, for all Israel had gone to Shechem to make him king. ² When Jeroboam son of Nebat heard about it—for he was in Egypt where he had fled from King Solomon's presence—Jeroboam returned from Egypt. ³ So they summoned him. Then Jeroboam and all Israel came and spoke to Rehoboam: ⁴ "Your father made our yoke harsh. Therefore, lighten your father's harsh service and the heavy yoke he put on us, and we will serve you."

⁵ Rehoboam replied, "Return to me in three days." So the people left.

⁶ Then King Rehoboam consulted with the elders who had attended his father Solomon when he was alive, asking, "How do you advise me to respond to this people?"

⁷ They replied, "If you will be kind to this people and please them by speaking kind words to them, they will be your servants forever."

⁸ But he rejected the advice of the elders who had advised him, and he consulted with the young men who had grown up with him, the ones attending him. ⁹ He asked them, "What message do you advise we send back to this people who said to me, 'Lighten the yoke your father put on us'?"

¹⁰ Then the young men who had grown up with him told him, "This is what you should say to the people who said to you, 'Your father made our yoke heavy, but you, make it lighter on us!' This is what you should say to them: 'My little finger is thicker than my father's waist! ¹¹ Now therefore, my father burdened you with a heavy yoke, but I will add to your yoke; my father disciplined you with whips, but I, with barbed whips.'"

¹² So Jeroboam and all the people came to Rehoboam on the third day, just as the king had ordered, saying, "Return to me on the third day." ¹³ Then the king answered them harshly. King Rehoboam rejected the elders' advice ¹⁴ and spoke to them according to the young men's advice,

WHO ARE THE KINGS LISTED IN MATTHEW'S GENEALOGY OF JESUS?

After David and Solomon, several kings are listed as Jesus's ancestors. In the books of 1 & 2 Kings and 1 & 2 Chronicles, the legacy of these kings are summarized as "evil" or doing what was "right in the LORD's sight"—or occasionally both (2Ch 12:14; 2Kg 18:3). These categories, however, do not necessarily describe every aspect of their lives; some kings displayed evil and faithfulness in both motive and action.

Rehoboam, Abijah, Joram, Ahaz, Manasseh, Amon, and Jeconiah are described as evil.

Asa, Jehoshaphat, Uzziah, Jotham, Hezekiah, and Josiah are all described as faithful to God.

saying, "My father made your yoke heavy, but I will add to it; my father disciplined you with whips, but I, with barbed whips."

¹⁵ The king did not listen to the people because the turn of events came from God, in order that the Lord might carry out his word that he had spoken through Ahijah the Shilonite to Jeroboam son of Nebat.

¹⁶ When all Israel saw that the king had not listened to them, the people answered the king:

> What portion do we have in David?
> We have no inheritance in the son of Jesse.
> Israel, each to your tent;
> David, look after your own house now!

So all Israel went to their tents. ¹⁷ But as for the Israelites living in the cities of Judah, Rehoboam reigned over them.

¹⁸ Then King Rehoboam sent Hadoram, who was in charge of the forced labor, but the Israelites stoned him to death. However, King Rehoboam managed to get into his chariot to flee to Jerusalem. ¹⁹ Israel is in rebellion against the house of David until today.

FROM CHAPTER 11

Rehoboam in Jerusalem

¹ When Rehoboam arrived in Jerusalem, he mobilized the house of Judah and Benjamin—one hundred eighty thousand fit young soldiers—to fight against Israel to restore the reign to Rehoboam. ² But the word of the Lord came to Shemaiah, the man of God: ³ "Say to Rehoboam son of Solomon, king of Judah, to all Israel in Judah and Benjamin, and to the rest of the people, ⁴ 'This is what the Lord says: You are not to march up and fight against your brothers. Each of you return home, for this incident has come from me.'"

So they listened to what the Lord said and turned back from going against Jeroboam.

Judah's King Rehoboam

⁵ Rehoboam stayed in Jerusalem, and he fortified cities in Judah. ⁶ He built up Bethlehem, Etam, Tekoa, ⁷ Beth-zur, Soco, Adullam, ⁸ Gath, Mareshah, Ziph, ⁹ Adoraim, Lachish, Azekah, ¹⁰ Zorah, Aijalon, and Hebron, which are fortified cities in Judah and in Benjamin. ¹¹ He strengthened their fortifications and put leaders in them with supplies of food, oil, and wine. ¹² He also put large shields and spears in each and every city to make them very strong. So Judah and Benjamin were his.

¹³ The priests and Levites from all their regions throughout Israel took their stand with Rehoboam, ¹⁴ for the Levites left their pasturelands and their possessions and went to Judah and Jerusalem, because Jeroboam and his sons refused to let them serve as priests of the LORD. ¹⁵ Jeroboam appointed his own priests for the high places, the goat-demons, and the golden calves he had made. ¹⁶ Those from every tribe of Israel who had determined in their hearts to seek the LORD their God followed the Levites to Jerusalem to sacrifice to the LORD, the God of their ancestors. ¹⁷ So they strengthened the kingdom of Judah and supported Rehoboam son of Solomon for three years, because they walked in the ways of David and Solomon for three years.

¹⁸ Rehoboam married Mahalath, daughter of David's son Jerimoth and of Abihail daughter of Jesse's son Eliab. ¹⁹ She bore sons to him: Jeush, Shemariah, and Zaham. ²⁰ After her, he married Maacah daughter of Absalom. She bore Abijah, Attai, Ziza, and Shelomith to him. ²¹ Rehoboam loved Maacah daughter of Absalom more than all his wives and concubines. He acquired eighteen wives and sixty concubines and was the father of twenty-eight sons and sixty daughters.

²² Rehoboam appointed Abijah son of Maacah as chief, leader among his brothers, intending to make him king. ²³ Rehoboam also showed discernment by dispersing some of his sons to all the regions of Judah and Benjamin and to all the fortified cities. He gave them plenty of provisions and sought many wives for them.

FROM CHAPTER 12

Shishak's Invasion

¹ When Rehoboam had established his sovereignty and royal power, he abandoned the law of the LORD—he and all Israel with him. ² Because they were unfaithful to the LORD, in the fifth year of King Rehoboam, King Shishak of Egypt went to war against Jerusalem ³ with 1,200 chariots, 60,000 cavalrymen, and countless people who came with him from Egypt—Libyans, Sukkiim, and Cushites. ⁴ He captured the fortified cities of Judah and came as far as Jerusalem.

⁵ Then the prophet Shemaiah went to Rehoboam and the leaders of Judah who were gathered at Jerusalem because of Shishak. He said to them, "This is what the LORD says: You have abandoned me; therefore, I have abandoned you to Shishak."

⁶ So the leaders of Israel and the king humbled themselves and said, "The LORD is righteous."

⁷ When the LORD saw that they had humbled themselves, the LORD's message came to Shemaiah: "They have humbled themselves; I will not destroy them but will grant them a little deliverance. My wrath will not be poured out on Jerusalem through Shishak. ⁸ However, they will become his servants so that they may recognize the difference between serving me and serving the kingdoms of other lands."

Notes

⁹ So King Shishak of Egypt went to war against Jerusalem. He seized the treasuries of the Lᴏʀᴅ's temple and the treasuries of the royal palace. He took everything. He took the gold shields that Solomon had made. ¹⁰ King Rehoboam made bronze shields to replace them and committed them into the care of the captains of the guards who protected the entrance to the king's palace. ¹¹ Whenever the king entered the Lᴏʀᴅ's temple, the guards would carry the shields and take them back to the armory.

¹² When Rehoboam humbled himself, the Lᴏʀᴅ's anger turned away from him, and he did not destroy him completely. Besides that, conditions were good in Judah.

Rehoboam's Last Days

¹³ King Rehoboam established his royal power in Jerusalem. Rehoboam was forty-one years old when he became king, and he reigned seventeen years in Jerusalem, the city the Lᴏʀᴅ had chosen from all the tribes of Israel to put his name. Rehoboam's mother's name was Naamah the Ammonite. ¹⁴ Rehoboam did what was evil, because he did not determine in his heart to seek the Lᴏʀᴅ.

¹⁵ The events of Rehoboam's reign, from beginning to end, are written in the Events of the Prophet Shemaiah and of the Seer Iddo concerning genealogies. There was war between Rehoboam and Jeroboam throughout their reigns. ¹⁶ Rehoboam rested with his ancestors and was buried in the city of David. His son Abijah became king in his place.

RESPONSE

01

What stood out to you
or surprised you about
Rehoboam's life?

02

From what you observed, how
would you describe Rehoboam's
relationship with God?

03

What did you relate to in
Rehoboam's story?

04

What connections did you see
in today's reading to the other
stories we've read?

AHAZ, THE KING PROMISED A SIGN

Ahaz was an evil and unfaithful king who worshiped other gods. He led the entire nation of Judah into the hands of their enemies. Despite his failures, he received a prophecy through Isaiah that the deliverer—Immanuel—would come from Ahaz's own family line.

2 KINGS

FROM CHAPTER 16

Judah's King Ahaz

¹ In the seventeenth year of Pekah son of Remaliah, Ahaz son of Jotham became king of Judah. ² Ahaz was twenty years old when he became king, and he reigned sixteen years in Jerusalem. He did not do what was right in the sight of the LORD his God like his ancestor David ³ but walked in the ways of the kings of Israel. He even sacrificed his son in the fire, imitating the detestable practices of the nations the LORD had dispossessed before the Israelites. ⁴ He sacrificed and burned incense on the high places, on the hills, and under every green tree.

⁵ Then Aram's King Rezin and Israel's King Pekah son of Remaliah came to wage war against Jerusalem. They besieged Ahaz but were not able to conquer him. ⁶ At that time Aram's King Rezin recovered Elath for Aram and expelled the Judahites from Elath. Then the Arameans came to Elath, and they still live there today.

⁷ So Ahaz sent messengers to King Tiglath-pileser of Assyria, saying, "I am your servant and your son. March up and save me from the grasp of the king of Aram and of the king of

Israel, who are rising up against me." [8] Ahaz also took the silver and gold found in the LORD's temple and in the treasuries of the king's palace and sent them to the king of Assyria as a bribe. [9] So the king of Assyria listened to him and marched up to Damascus and captured it. He deported its people to Kir but put Rezin to death.

Ahaz's Idolatry

[10] King Ahaz went to Damascus to meet King Tiglath-pileser of Assyria. When he saw the altar that was in Damascus, King Ahaz sent a model of the altar and complete plans for its construction to the priest Uriah. [11] Uriah built the altar according to all the instructions King Ahaz sent from Damascus. Therefore, by the time King Ahaz came back from Damascus, the priest Uriah had completed it. [12] When the king came back from Damascus, he saw the altar. Then he approached the altar and ascended it. [13] He offered his burnt offering and his grain offering, poured out his drink offering, and splattered the blood of his fellowship offerings on the altar. [14] He took the bronze altar that was before the LORD in front of the temple between his altar and the LORD's temple, and put it on the north side of his altar.

[15] Then King Ahaz commanded the priest Uriah, "Offer on the great altar the morning burnt offering, the evening grain offering, and the king's burnt offering and his grain offering. Also offer the burnt offering of all the people of the land, their grain offering, and their drink offerings. Splatter on the altar all the blood of the burnt offering and all the blood of sacrifice. The bronze altar will be for me to seek guidance." [16] The priest Uriah did everything King Ahaz commanded.

[17] Then King Ahaz cut off the frames of the water carts and removed the bronze basin from each of them. He took the basin from the bronze oxen that were under it and put it on a stone pavement. [18] To satisfy the king of Assyria, he removed from the LORD's temple the Sabbath canopy they had built in the palace, and he closed the outer entrance for the king.

2 CHRONICLES

FROM CHAPTER 28

[21] Although Ahaz plundered the LORD's temple and the palace of the king and of the rulers and gave the plunder to the king of Assyria, it did not help him.

[22] At the time of his distress, King Ahaz himself became more unfaithful to the LORD. [23] He sacrificed to the gods of Damascus which had defeated him; he said, "Since the gods of the kings of Aram are helping them, I will sacrifice to them so that they will help me." But they were the downfall of him and of all Israel.

[24] Then Ahaz gathered up the utensils of God's temple, cut them into pieces, shut the doors of the LORD's temple, and made himself altars on every street corner in

Notes

Jerusalem. ²⁵ He made high places in every city of Judah to offer incense to other gods, and he angered the LORD, the God of his ancestors.

ISAIAH

FROM CHAPTER 7

The Immanuel Prophecy

¹⁰ Then the LORD spoke again to Ahaz: ¹¹ "Ask for a sign from the LORD your God—it can be as deep as Sheol or as high as heaven."

¹² But Ahaz replied, "I will not ask. I will not test the LORD."

¹³ Isaiah said, "Listen, house of David! Is it not enough for you to try the patience of men? Will you also try the patience of my God?

¹⁴ Therefore, the Lord himself will give you a sign: See, the virgin will conceive, have a son, and name him Immanuel.

¹⁵ By the time he learns to reject what is bad and choose what is good, he will be eating curds and honey. ¹⁶ For before the boy knows to reject what is bad and choose what is good, the land of the two kings you dread will be abandoned. ¹⁷ The LORD will bring on you, your people, and your father's house such a time as has never been since Ephraim separated from Judah: He will bring the king of Assyria."

¹⁸ On that day
the LORD will whistle to flies
at the farthest streams of the Nile
and to bees in the land of Assyria.
¹⁹ All of them will come and settle
in the steep ravines, in the clefts of the rocks,
in all the thornbushes, and in all the water holes.

²⁰ On that day the Lord will use a razor hired from beyond the Euphrates River—the king of Assyria—to shave the hair on your heads, the hair on your legs, and even your beards.

²¹ On that day
a man will raise a young cow and two sheep,
²² and from the abundant milk they give
he will eat curds,
for every survivor in the land will eat curds and honey.

²³ And on that day
every place where there were a thousand vines,
worth a thousand pieces of silver,
will become thorns and briers.
²⁴ A man will go there with bow and arrows
because the whole land will be thorns and briers.
²⁵ You will not go to all the hills
that were once tilled with a hoe,
for fear of the thorns and briers.
Those hills will be places for oxen to graze
and for sheep to trample.

RESPONSE

01
_____

What stood out to you or
surprised you about Ahaz's life?

02
_____

From what you observed,
how would you describe Ahaz's
relationship with God?

03
_____

What did you relate to in
Ahaz's story?

04
_____

What connections did you see
in today's reading to the other
stories we've read?

POTHOS PLANT PROPAGATION

SUPPLIES

- Pothos plant
  any variety works for this method
- Garden shears or scissors
- Glass container
- Soil
- Pot

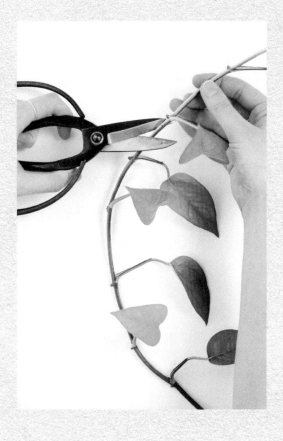

INSTRUCTIONS

Cut off approximately 6 inches of your pothos stem. Make the cut right below a root node—one of the small brown bumps on the stem. (The new plant roots will grow from this node.)

Cut off any leaves that will be submerged in water, leaving two to three leaves at the top of the stem.

Fill your glass container with room temperature water. Place the cutting in water, making sure at least one of the nodes is submerged.

Place your glass container in a well-lit area, since roots will grow fastest in this type of setting.

When the roots are about 1 inch long, you can remove the clipping from the water and plant it directly in soil in a pot of your choosing. When potting your new plant, make sure all of the new roots are completely covered with soil.

Enjoy your new plant!

SOME VARIETIES OF POTHOS PLANTS

Global Green   Neon   Pearls and Jade   Golden   Marble Queen

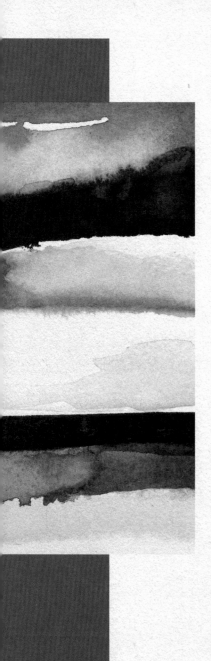

HEZEKIAH, REFORMER AND RESTORER

Hezekiah was the twelfth king of Judah. He reoriented the people back to true worship by cleansing the temple, reinstating the Passover, and reestablishing the priesthood. God answered his prayer to deliver Jerusalem from the hands of their enemy, Assyria.

Keep paying attention to themes of inheritance, legacy, and place as you read! Turn back to page 46 for a refresher.

2 KINGS

FROM CHAPTER 18

Judah's King Hezekiah

[1] In the third year of Israel's King Hoshea son of Elah, Hezekiah son of Ahaz became king of Judah. [2] He was twenty-five years old when he became king, and he reigned twenty-nine years in Jerusalem. His mother's name was Abi daughter of Zechariah. [3] He did what was right in the LORD's sight just as his ancestor David had done. [4] He removed the high places, shattered the sacred pillars, and cut down the Asherah poles. He broke into pieces the bronze snake that Moses made, for until then the Israelites were burning incense to it. It was called Nehushtan.

[5] Hezekiah relied on the LORD God of Israel; not one of the kings of Judah was like him, either before him or after him. [6] He remained faithful to the LORD and did not turn from following him but kept the commands the LORD had commanded Moses.

[7] The LORD was with him, and wherever he went he prospered. He rebelled against the king of Assyria and did not serve him. [8] He defeated the Philistines as far as Gaza and its borders, from watchtower to fortified city.

2 CHRONICLES

FROM CHAPTER 29

[3] In the first year of his reign, in the first month, he opened the doors of the Lord's temple and repaired them. [4] Then he brought in the priests and Levites and gathered them in the eastern public square. [5] He said to them, "Hear me, Levites. Consecrate yourselves now and consecrate the temple of the Lord, the God of your ancestors. Remove everything impure from the holy place. [6] For our ancestors were unfaithful and did what is evil in the sight of the Lord our God. They abandoned him, turned their faces away from the Lord's dwelling place, and turned their backs on him. [7] They also closed the doors of the portico, extinguished the lamps, did not burn incense, and did not offer burnt offerings in the holy place of the God of Israel. [8] Therefore, the wrath of the Lord was on Judah and Jerusalem, and he made them an object of terror, horror, and mockery, as you see with your own eyes. [9] Our fathers fell by the sword, and our sons, our daughters, and our wives are in captivity because of this. [10] It is in my heart now to make a covenant with the Lord, the God of Israel so that his burning anger may turn away from us. [11] My sons, don't be negligent now, for

the Lord has chosen you to stand in his presence,

to serve him, and to be his ministers and burners of incense."

FROM CHAPTER 30

Celebration of the Passover

[1] Then Hezekiah sent word throughout all Israel and Judah, and he also wrote letters to Ephraim and Manasseh to come to the Lord's temple in Jerusalem to observe the Passover of the Lord, the God of Israel. [2] For the king and his officials and the entire congregation in Jerusalem decided to observe the Passover of the Lord in the second month, [3] because they were not able to observe it at the appropriate time. Not enough of the priests had consecrated themselves, and the people hadn't been gathered together in Jerusalem. [4] The proposal pleased the king and the congregation, [5] so they affirmed the proposal and spread the message throughout all Israel, from Beer-sheba to Dan, to come to observe the Passover of the Lord, the God of Israel in Jerusalem, for they hadn't observed it often, as prescribed.

[6] So the couriers went throughout Israel and Judah with letters from the hand of the king and his officials, and according to the king's command, saying, "Israelites, return to the Lord, the God of Abraham, Isaac, and Israel so that he may return to those of you who remain, who have escaped the grasp of the kings of Assyria. [7] Don't be like your ancestors and your brothers who were unfaithful to the Lord, the God of their ancestors so that he made them an object of horror as you yourselves see."

Notes

Removal of Idolatry

[1] When all this was completed, all Israel who had attended went out to the cities of Judah and broke up the sacred pillars, chopped down the Asherah poles, and tore down the high places and altars throughout Judah and Benjamin, as well as in Ephraim and Manasseh, to the last one. Then all the Israelites returned to their cities, each to his own possession.

Offerings for Levites

[2] Hezekiah reestablished the divisions of the priests and Levites for the burnt offerings and fellowship offerings, for ministry, for giving thanks, and for praise in the gates of the camp of the LORD, each division corresponding to his service among the priests and Levites. [3] The king contributed from his own possessions for the regular morning and evening burnt offerings, the burnt offerings of the Sabbaths, of the New Moons, and of the appointed feasts, as written in the law of the LORD. [4] He told the people who lived in Jerusalem to give a contribution for the priests and Levites so that they could devote their energy to the law of the LORD. [5] When the word spread, the Israelites gave liberally of the best of the grain, new wine, fresh oil, honey, and of all the produce of the field, and they brought in an abundance, a tenth of everything. [6] As for the Israelites and Judahites who lived in the cities of Judah, they also brought a tenth of the herds and flocks, and a tenth of the dedicated things that were consecrated to the LORD their God. They gathered them into large piles. [7] In the third month they began building up the piles, and they finished in the seventh month. [8] When Hezekiah and his officials came and viewed the piles, they blessed the LORD and his people Israel.

…

[20] Hezekiah did this throughout all Judah. He did what was good and upright and true before the LORD his God. [21] He was diligent in every deed that he began in the service of God's temple, in the instruction and the commands, in order to seek his God, and he prospered.

RESPONSE

01

What stood out to you
or surprised you about
Hezekiah's life?

02

From what you observed, how
would you describe Hezekiah's
relationship with God?

03

What did you relate to in
Hezekiah's story?

04

What connections did you see
in today's reading to the other
stories we've read?

MANASSEH, ENCOURAGER OF EVIL

Manasseh reinstituted the evil practices that his father, Hezekiah, worked to remove from Judah, including corrupt religious practices and social injustices. Though Manasseh later repented, God still promised to bring about the exile of the people of Judah because of Manasseh's personal sin and the sin he led the people of Judah to commit.

2 KINGS

FROM CHAPTER 21

Judah's King Manasseh

¹ Manasseh was twelve years old when he became king, and he reigned fifty-five years in Jerusalem. His mother's name was Hephzibah. ² He did what was evil in the LORD's sight, imitating the detestable practices of the nations that the LORD had dispossessed before the Israelites. ³ He rebuilt the high places that his father Hezekiah had destroyed and reestablished the altars for Baal. He made an Asherah, as King Ahab of Israel had done; he also bowed in worship to all the stars in the sky and served them. ⁴ He built altars in the LORD's temple, where the LORD had said, "Jerusalem is where I will put my name." ⁵ He built altars to all the stars in the sky in both courtyards of the LORD's temple. ⁶ He sacrificed his son in the fire, practiced witchcraft and divination, and consulted mediums and spiritists. He did a huge amount of evil in the LORD's sight, angering him.

⁷ Manasseh set up the carved image of Asherah, which he made, in the temple that the LORD had spoken about to David and his son Solomon: "I will establish my name forever in this temple and in Jerusalem, which I have chosen out of all the tribes of Israel. ⁸ I will never again cause the feet of the Israelites to wander from the land I gave to their ancestors if only they will be careful to do all I have commanded them—the whole law that my servant Moses commanded

them." ⁹ But they did not listen; Manasseh caused them to stray so that they did worse evil than the nations the LORD had destroyed before the Israelites.

¹⁰ The LORD said through his servants the prophets, ¹¹ "Since King Manasseh of Judah has committed all these detestable acts—worse evil than the Amorites who preceded him had done—and by means of his idols has also caused Judah to sin, ¹² this is what the LORD God of Israel says: 'I am about to bring such a disaster on Jerusalem and Judah that everyone who hears about it will shudder. ¹³ I will stretch over Jerusalem the measuring line used on Samaria and the mason's level used on the house of Ahab, and I will wipe Jerusalem clean as one wipes a bowl—wiping it and turning it upside down. ¹⁴ I will abandon the remnant of my inheritance and hand them over to their enemies. They will become plunder and spoil to all their enemies, ¹⁵ because they have done what is evil in my sight and have angered me from the day their ancestors came out of Egypt until today.'"

¹⁶ Manasseh also shed so much innocent blood that he filled Jerusalem with it from one end to another. This was in addition to his sin that he caused Judah to commit, so that they did what was evil in the LORD's sight.

²⁶ In spite of all that, the LORD did not turn from the fury of his intense burning anger, which burned against Judah because of all the affronts with which Manasseh had angered him. ²⁷ For the LORD had said, "I will also remove Judah from my presence just as I have removed Israel. I will reject this city Jerusalem, that I have chosen, and the temple about which I said, 'My name will be there.'"

JEREMIAH

FROM CHAPTER 15

The Lord's Negative Response

¹ Then the LORD said to me, "Even if Moses and Samuel should stand before me, my compassions would not reach out to these people. Send them from my presence, and let them go. ² If they ask you, 'Where will we go?' tell them: This is what the LORD says:

> Those destined for death, to death;
> those destined for the sword, to the sword.
> Those destined for famine, to famine;
> those destined for captivity, to captivity.

³ "I will ordain four kinds of judgment for them"—this is the LORD's declaration—"the sword to kill, the dogs to drag away, and the birds of the sky and the wild animals of the land to devour and destroy. ⁴ I will make them a horror to all the kingdoms of the earth because of Manasseh son of Hezekiah, the king of Judah, for what he did in Jerusalem."

2 CHRONICLES

FROM CHAPTER 33

Manasseh's Repentance

¹⁰ The LORD spoke to Manasseh and his people, but they didn't listen. ¹¹ So he brought against them the military commanders of the king of Assyria. They captured Manasseh with hooks, bound him with bronze shackles, and took him to Babylon.

¹² When he was in distress, he sought the favor of the LORD his God and earnestly humbled himself before the God of his ancestors.

¹³ He prayed to him, and the LORD was receptive to his prayer. He granted his request and brought him back to Jerusalem, to his kingdom. So Manasseh came to know that the LORD is God.

¹⁴ After this, he built the outer wall of the city of David from west of Gihon in the valley to the entrance of the Fish Gate; he brought it around Ophel, and he heightened it considerably. He also placed military commanders in all the fortified cities of Judah.

¹⁵ He removed the foreign gods and the idol from the LORD's temple, along with all the altars that he had built on the mountain of the LORD's temple and in Jerusalem, and he threw them outside the city. ¹⁶ He built the altar of the LORD and offered fellowship and thanksgiving sacrifices on it. Then he told Judah to serve the LORD, the God of Israel. ¹⁷ However, the people still sacrificed at the high places, but only to the LORD their God.

RESPONSE

01

What stood out to you
or surprised you about
Manasseh's life?

02

From what you observed, how
would you describe Manasseh's
relationship with God?

03

What did you relate to in
Manasseh's story?

04

What connections did you see
in today's reading to the other
stories we've read?

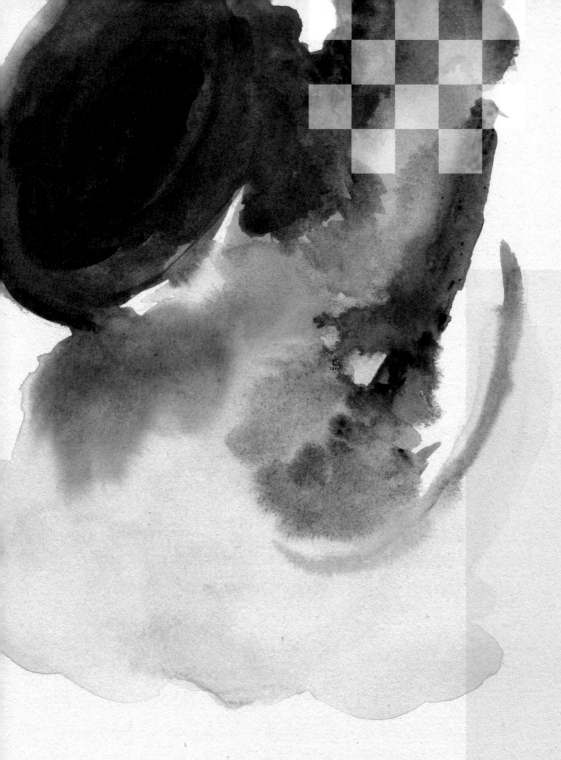

GRACE DAY

Take this day to catch up on your reading, pray, and rest in the presence of the Lord.

THEREFORE, THE LORD HIMSELF WILL GIVE YOU A SIGN: SEE, THE VIRGIN WILL CONCEIVE, HAVE A SON, AND NAME HIM IMMANUEL.

ISAIAH 7:14

Scripture is God-breathed and true. When we memorize it,
we carry the good news of Jesus with us wherever we go.

We'll add verse 17, to finish up our memorization of Romans 8:14-17.
It's a reminder that, as God's children, we are also coheirs with Christ.

¹⁴ FOR ALL THOSE LED BY GOD'S SPIRIT ARE
GOD'S SONS. ¹⁵ FOR YOU DID NOT RECEIVE
A SPIRIT OF SLAVERY TO FALL BACK INTO
FEAR. INSTEAD, YOU RECEIVED THE SPIRIT OF
ADOPTION, BY WHOM WE CRY OUT, "*ABBA*,
FATHER!" ¹⁶ THE SPIRIT HIMSELF TESTIFIES
TOGETHER WITH OUR SPIRIT THAT WE ARE
GOD'S CHILDREN, ¹⁷ AND IF CHILDREN, ALSO
HEIRS—HEIRS OF GOD AND COHEIRS WITH
CHRIST—IF INDEED WE SUFFER WITH HIM SO
THAT WE MAY ALSO BE GLORIFIED WITH HIM.

ROMANS 8:14-17

See tips for memorizing Scripture on page 172.

Day 29

JOSIAH, WHO HEARD THE UNEARTHED WORD OF GOD

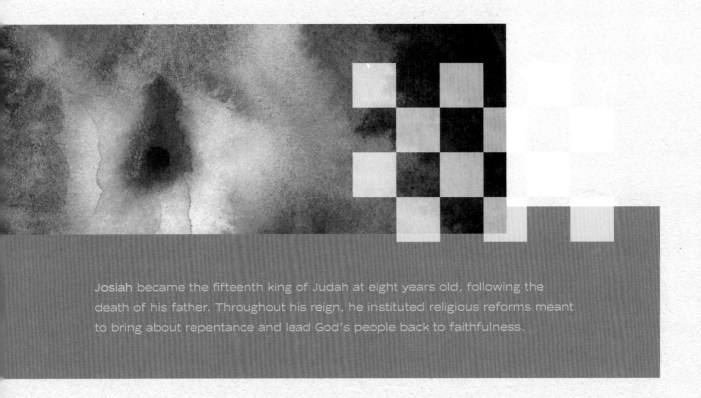

Josiah became the fifteenth king of Judah at eight years old, following the death of his father. Throughout his reign, he instituted religious reforms meant to bring about repentance and lead God's people back to faithfulness.

2 KINGS

FROM CHAPTER 21

Judah's King Amon

¹⁹ Amon was twenty-two years old when he became king, and he reigned two years in Jerusalem. His mother's name was Meshullemeth daughter of Haruz; she was from Jotbah. ²⁰ He did what was evil in the LORD's sight, just as his father Manasseh had done. ²¹ He walked in all the ways his father had walked; he served the idols his father had served, and he bowed in worship to them. ²² He abandoned the LORD God of his ancestors and did not walk in the ways of the LORD.

²³ Amon's servants conspired against him and put the king to death in his own house. ²⁴ The common people killed all who had conspired against King Amon, and they made his son Josiah king in his place.

²⁵ The rest of the events of Amon's reign, along with his accomplishments, are written in the Historical Record of Judah's Kings.

Judah's King Josiah

[1] Josiah was eight years old when he became king, and he reigned thirty-one years in Jerusalem. His mother's name was Jedidah the daughter of Adaiah; she was from Bozkath. [2] He did what was right in the LORD's sight and walked in all the ways of his ancestor David; he did not turn to the right or the left.

Josiah Repairs the Temple

[3] In the eighteenth year of King Josiah, the king sent the court secretary Shaphan son of Azaliah, son of Meshullam, to the LORD's temple, saying, [4] "Go up to the high priest Hilkiah so that he may total up the silver brought into the LORD's temple—the silver the doorkeepers have collected from the people. [5] It is to be given to those doing the work—those who oversee the LORD's temple. They in turn are to give it to the workmen in the LORD's temple to repair the damage. [6] They are to give it to the carpenters, builders, and masons to buy timber and quarried stone to repair the temple. [7] But no accounting is to be required from them for the silver given to them since they work with integrity."

The Book of the Law Found

[8] The high priest Hilkiah told the court secretary Shaphan, "I have found the book of the law in the LORD's temple," and he gave the book to Shaphan, who read it.

[9] Then the court secretary Shaphan went to the king and reported, "Your servants have emptied out the silver that was found in the temple and have given it to those doing the work—those who oversee the LORD's temple." [10] Then the court secretary Shaphan told the king, "The priest Hilkiah has given me a book," and Shaphan read it in the presence of the king.

[11] When the king heard the words of the book of the law, he tore his clothes. [12] Then he commanded the priest Hilkiah, Ahikam son of Shaphan, Achbor son of Micaiah, the court secretary Shaphan, and the king's servant Asaiah, [13] "Go and inquire of the LORD for me, for the people, and for all Judah about the words in this book that has been found. For great is the LORD's wrath that is kindled against us because our ancestors have not obeyed the words of this book in order to do everything written about us."

Huldah's Prophecy of Judgment

[14] So the priest Hilkiah, Ahikam, Achbor, Shaphan, and Asaiah went to the prophetess Huldah, wife of Shallum son of Tikvah, son of Harhas, keeper of the wardrobe. She lived in Jerusalem in the Second District. They spoke with her.

[15] She said to them, "This is what the LORD God of Israel says: Say to the man who sent you to me, [16] 'This is what the LORD says: I am about to bring disaster on this

Notes

place and on its inhabitants, fulfilling all the words of the book that the king of Judah has read, [17] because they have abandoned me and burned incense to other gods in order to anger me with all the work of their hands. My wrath will be kindled against this place, and it will not be quenched.' [18] Say this to the king of Judah who sent you to inquire of the LORD: 'This is what the LORD God of Israel says: As for the words that you heard,

[19] because your heart was tender and you humbled yourself before the LORD

when you heard what I spoke against this place and against its inhabitants, that they would become a desolation and a curse, and because you have torn your clothes and wept before me, I myself have heard'—this is the LORD's declaration. [20] 'Therefore, I will indeed gather you to your ancestors, and you will be gathered to your grave in peace. Your eyes will not see all the disaster that I am bringing on this place.'"

Then they reported to the king.

FROM CHAPTER 23

Covenant Renewal

[1] So the king sent messengers, and they gathered all the elders of Judah and Jerusalem to him. [2] Then the king went to the LORD's temple with all the men of Judah and all the inhabitants of Jerusalem, as well as the priests and the prophets—all the people from the youngest to the oldest. He read in their hearing all the words of the book of the covenant that had been found in the LORD's temple. [3] Next, the king stood by the pillar and made a covenant in the LORD's presence to follow the LORD and to keep his commands, his decrees, and his statutes with all his heart and with all his soul in order to carry out the words of this covenant that were written in this book; all the people agreed to the covenant.

…

Further Zeal for the Lord

[24] In addition, Josiah eradicated the mediums, the spiritists, household idols, images, and all the abhorrent things that were seen in the land of Judah and in Jerusalem. He did this in order to carry out the words of the law that were written in the book that the priest Hilkiah found in the LORD's temple. [25] Before him there was no king like him who turned to the LORD with all his heart and with all his soul and with all his strength according to all the law of Moses, and no one like him arose after him.

[26] In spite of all that, the LORD did not turn from the fury of his intense burning anger, which burned against Judah because of all the affronts with which Manasseh had angered him. [27] For the LORD had said, "I will also remove Judah from my presence just as I have removed Israel. I will reject this city Jerusalem, that I have chosen, and the temple about which I said, 'My name will be there.'"

Josiah's Death

[28] The rest of the events of Josiah's reign, along with all his accomplishments, are written in the Historical Record of Judah's Kings. [29] During his reign, Pharaoh Neco king of Egypt marched up to help the king of Assyria at the Euphrates River. King Josiah went to confront him, and at Megiddo when Neco saw him he killed him. [30] From Megiddo his servants carried his dead body in a chariot, brought him into Jerusalem, and buried him in his own tomb. Then the common people took Jehoahaz son of Josiah, anointed him, and made him king in place of his father.

01

What stood out to you or
surprised you about Josiah's life?

02

From what you observed, how
would you describe Josiah's
relationship with God?

03

What did you relate to in
Josiah's story?

04

What connections did you see
in today's reading to the other
stories we've read?

ZERUBBABEL, REBUILDER OF RUINS

Under the reign of Josiah's descendant Zedekiah,
King Nebuchadnezzar destroyed Jerusalem and the temple
and carried the last group of Jewish people to Babylon. They
remained in exile for seventy years, then were allowed to return
to their homeland. During this period of return, Zerubbabel,
Josiah's descendant, served as the governor of Judah and
helped rebuild the temple in Jerusalem.

HAGGAI

FROM CHAPTER 1

Command to Rebuild the Temple

¹ In the second year of King Darius, on the first day of the sixth month, the word of the LORD came through the prophet Haggai to Zerubbabel son of Shealtiel, the governor of Judah, and to Joshua son of Jehozadak, the high priest:

² "The LORD of Armies says this: These people say: The time has not come for the house of the LORD to be rebuilt."

³ The word of the LORD came through the prophet Haggai: ⁴ "Is it a time for you yourselves to live in your paneled houses, while this house lies in ruins?" ⁵ Now, the LORD of Armies says this: "Think carefully about your ways:

⁶ You have planted much
but harvested little.
You eat
but never have enough to be satisfied.
You drink
but never have enough to be happy.
You put on clothes
but never have enough to get warm.
The wage earner puts his wages
into a bag with a hole in it."

⁷ The LORD of Armies says this: "Think carefully about your ways. ⁸ Go up into the hills, bring down lumber, and build the house; and I will be pleased with it and be glorified," says the LORD. ⁹ "You expected much, but then it amounted to little. When you brought the harvest to your house, I ruined it. Why?" This is the declaration of the LORD of Armies. "Because my house still lies in ruins, while each of you is busy with his own house.

¹⁰ So on your account,
the skies have withheld the dew

and the land its crops.
¹¹ I have summoned a drought
on the fields and the hills,
on the grain, new wine, fresh oil,
and whatever the ground yields,
on people and animals,
and on all that your hands produce."

The People's Response

¹² Then Zerubbabel son of Shealtiel, the high priest Joshua son of Jehozadak, and the entire remnant of the people obeyed the LORD their God and the words of the prophet Haggai, because the LORD their God had sent him. So the people feared the LORD.

¹³ Then Haggai, the LORD's messenger, delivered the LORD's message to the people:

"I am with you—this is the
LORD's declaration."

¹⁴ The LORD roused the spirit of Zerubbabel son of Shealtiel, governor of Judah, the spirit of the high priest Joshua son of Jehozadak, and the spirit of all the remnant of the people. They began work on the house of the LORD of Armies, their God, ¹⁵ on the twenty-fourth day of the sixth month, in the second year of King Darius.

FROM CHAPTER 2

Encouragement and Promise

¹ On the twenty-first day of the seventh month, the word of the LORD came through the prophet Haggai: ² "Speak to Zerubbabel son of Shealtiel, governor of Judah, to the high priest Joshua son of Jehozadak, and to the remnant of the

people: [3] 'Who is left among you who saw this house in its former glory? How does it look to you now? Doesn't it seem to you like nothing by comparison? [4] Even so, be strong, Zerubbabel—this is the LORD's declaration. Be strong, Joshua son of Jehozadak, high priest. Be strong, all you people of the land—this is the LORD's declaration. Work! For I am with you—the declaration of the LORD of Armies. [5] This is the promise I made to you when you came out of Egypt, and my Spirit is present among you; don't be afraid.'"

[6] For the LORD of Armies says this: "Once more, in a little while, I am going to shake the heavens and the earth, the sea and the dry land. [7] I will shake all the nations so that the treasures of all the nations will come, and I will fill this house with glory," says the LORD of Armies. [8] "The silver and gold belong to me"—this is the declaration of the LORD of Armies. [9] "The final glory of this house will be greater than the first," says the LORD of Armies. "I will provide peace in this place"—this is the declaration of the LORD of Armies.

From Deprivation to Blessing

[10] On the twenty-fourth day of the ninth month, in the second year of Darius, the word of the LORD came to the prophet Haggai: [11] "This is what the LORD of Armies says: Ask the priests for a ruling. [12] If a man is carrying consecrated meat in the fold of his garment, and it touches bread, stew, wine, oil, or any other food, does it become holy?"

The priests answered, "No."

[13] Then Haggai asked, "If someone defiled by contact with a corpse touches any of these, does it become defiled?"

The priests answered, "It becomes defiled."

[14] Then Haggai replied, "So is this people, and so is this nation before me—this is the LORD's declaration. And so is every work of their hands; even what they offer there is defiled.

[15] "Now from this day on, think carefully: Before one stone was placed on another in the LORD's temple, [16] what state were you in? When someone came to a grain heap of twenty measures, it only amounted to ten; when one came to the winepress to dip fifty measures from the vat, it only amounted to twenty. [17] I struck you—all the work of your hands—with blight, mildew, and hail, but you didn't turn to me—this is the LORD's declaration. [18] From this day on, think carefully; from the twenty-fourth day of the ninth month, from the day the foundation of the LORD's temple was laid; think carefully. [19] Is there still seed left in the granary? The vine, the fig, the pomegranate, and the olive tree have not yet produced. But from this day on I will bless you."

Promise to Zerubbabel

[20] The word of the LORD came to Haggai a second time on the twenty-fourth day of the month: [21] "Speak to Zerubbabel, governor of Judah: I am going to shake the heavens and the earth. [22] I will overturn royal thrones and destroy the power of the Gentile kingdoms. I will overturn chariots and their riders. Horses and their riders will fall, each by his brother's sword. [23] On that day"—this is the declaration of the LORD of Armies—"I will take you, Zerubbabel son of Shealtiel, my servant"—this is the LORD's declaration—"and make you like my signet ring, for I have chosen you." This is the declaration of the LORD of Armies.

RESPONSE

01

What stood out to you
or surprised you about
Zerubbabel's life?

02

From what you observed, how
would you describe Zerubbabel's
relationship with God?

03

What did you relate to in
Zerubbabel's story?

04

What connections did you see
in today's reading to the other
stories we've read?

JOSEPH, HUSBAND OF MARY

Joseph was the husband of Mary and the adoptive earthly father of Jesus. Joseph appears mostly in the narratives surrounding Jesus's birth and adolescence; the Gospels also tell us that he was the father of several other children through Mary and was a carpenter by trade.

MATTHEW

FROM CHAPTER 1

The Nativity of the Messiah

¹⁸ The birth of Jesus Christ came about this way: After his mother Mary had been engaged to Joseph, it was discovered before they came together that she was pregnant from the Holy Spirit. ¹⁹ So her husband, Joseph, being a righteous man, and not wanting to disgrace her publicly, decided to divorce her secretly.

²⁰ But after he had considered these things, an angel of the Lord appeared to him in a dream, saying, "Joseph, son of David, don't be afraid to take Mary as your wife, because what has been conceived in her is from the Holy Spirit. ²¹ She will give birth to a son, and you are to name him Jesus, because he will save his people from their sins."

²² Now all this took place to fulfill what was spoken by the Lord through the prophet:

²³ See, the virgin will become pregnant
and give birth to a son,
and they will name him Immanuel,

which is translated "God is with us."

²⁴ When Joseph woke up, he did as the Lord's angel had commanded him. He married her ²⁵ but did not have sexual relations with her until she gave birth to a son. And he named him Jesus.

FROM CHAPTER 2

Wise Men Visit the King

¹ After Jesus was born in Bethlehem of Judea in the days of King Herod, wise men from the east arrived in Jerusalem, ² saying, "Where is he who has been born king of the Jews? For we saw his star at its rising and have come to worship him."

³ When King Herod heard this, he was deeply disturbed, and all Jerusalem with him. ⁴ So he assembled all the chief priests and scribes of the people and asked them where the Messiah would be born.

⁵ "In Bethlehem of Judea," they told him, "because this is what was written by the prophet:

⁶ And you, Bethlehem, in the land of Judah,
are by no means least among the rulers of Judah:
Because out of you will come a ruler
who will shepherd my people Israel."

⁷ Then Herod secretly summoned the wise men and asked them the exact time the star appeared. ⁸ He sent them to Bethlehem and said, "Go and search carefully for the child. When you find him, report back to me so that I too can go and worship him."

⁹ After hearing the king, they went on their way. And there it was—the star they had seen at its rising. It led them until it came and stopped above the place where the child was.

[10] When they saw the star, they were overwhelmed with joy. [11] Entering the house, they saw the child with Mary his mother, and falling to their knees, they worshiped him. Then they opened their treasures and presented him with gifts: gold, frankincense, and myrrh. [12] And being warned in a dream not to go back to Herod, they returned to their own country by another route.

The Flight into Egypt

[13] After they were gone, an angel of the Lord appeared to Joseph in a dream, saying, "Get up! Take the child and his mother, flee to Egypt, and stay there until I tell you. For Herod is about to search for the child to kill him." [14] So he got up, took the child and his mother during the night, and escaped to Egypt. [15] He stayed there until Herod's death, so that what was spoken by the Lord through the prophet might be fulfilled: Out of Egypt I called my Son.

The Massacre of the Innocents

[16] Then Herod, when he realized that he had been outwitted by the wise men, flew into a rage. He gave orders to massacre all the boys in and around Bethlehem who were two years old and under, in keeping with the time he had learned from the wise men. [17] Then what was spoken through Jeremiah the prophet was fulfilled:

[18] A voice was heard in Ramah,

> weeping, and great mourning,
> Rachel weeping for her children;
> and she refused to be consoled,
> because they are no more.

The Return to Nazareth

[19] After Herod died, an angel of the Lord appeared in a dream to Joseph in Egypt, [20] saying, "Get up, take the child and his mother, and go to the land of Israel, because those who intended to kill the child are dead." [21] So he got up, took the child and his mother, and entered the land of Israel. [22] But when he heard that Archelaus was ruling over Judea in place of his father Herod, he was afraid to go there. And being warned in a dream, he withdrew to the region of Galilee. [23] Then he went and settled in a town called Nazareth to fulfill what was spoken through the prophets, that he would be called a Nazarene.

LUKE

FROM CHAPTER 2

In His Father's House

[41] Every year his parents traveled to Jerusalem for the Passover Festival. [42] When he was twelve years old, they went up according to the custom of the festival. [43] After those days were over, as they were returning, the boy Jesus stayed behind in Jerusalem, but his parents did not know it. [44] Assuming he was in the traveling party, they went a day's journey. Then they began looking for him among their relatives and friends. [45] When they did not find him, they returned to Jerusalem to search for him. [46] After three days, they found him in the temple sitting among the teachers, listening to them and asking them questions. [47] And all those who heard him were astounded at his understanding and his answers. [48] When his parents saw him, they were astonished, and his mother said to him, "Son, why have you treated us like this? Your father and I have been anxiously searching for you."

[49] "Why were you searching for me?" he asked them. "Didn't you know that it was necessary for me to be in my Father's house?" [50] But they did not understand what he said to them.

MATTHEW

FROM CHAPTER 13

Rejection at Nazareth

[53] When Jesus had finished these parables, he left there. [54] He went to his hometown and began to teach them in their synagogue, so that they were astonished and said, "Where did this man get this wisdom and these miraculous powers? [55] Isn't this the carpenter's son? Isn't his mother called Mary, and his brothers James, Joseph, Simon, and Judas? [56] And his sisters, aren't they all with us? So where does he get all these things?" [57] And they were offended by him.

Jesus said to them, "A prophet is not without honor except in his hometown and in his household." [58] And he did not do many miracles there because of their unbelief.

RESPONSE

01

What stood out to you or surprised you about Joseph's life?

02

From what you observed, how would you describe Joseph's relationship with God?

03

What did you relate to in Joseph's story?

04

What connections did you see in today's reading to the other stories we've read?

MARY, BLESSED AMONG WOMEN

Mary was the mother of Jesus and the wife of Joseph. She had more children with Joseph after Jesus, making Him the eldest of several sisters and brothers. Mary is present at key moments in Jesus's life and ministry, including His first miracle and His crucifixion. She also remained faithful to Jesus's mission after His death, resurrection, and ascension.

LUKE

FROM CHAPTER 1

Gabriel Predicts Jesus's Birth

²⁶ In the sixth month, the angel Gabriel was sent by God to a town in Galilee called Nazareth, ²⁷ to a virgin engaged to a man named Joseph, of the house of David. The virgin's name was Mary. ²⁸ And the angel came to her and said, "Greetings, favored woman! The Lord is with you." ²⁹ But she was deeply troubled by this statement, wondering what kind of greeting this could be. ³⁰ Then the angel told her, "Do not be afraid, Mary, for you have found favor with God. ³¹ Now listen:

You will conceive and give birth to a son, and you will name him Jesus. ³² He will be great and will be called the Son of the Most High, and the Lord God will give him the throne of his father David.

³³ He will reign over the house of Jacob forever, and his kingdom will have no end."

³⁴ Mary asked the angel, "How can this be, since I have not had sexual relations with a man?"

³⁵ The angel replied to her, "The Holy Spirit will come upon you, and the power of the Most High will overshadow you. Therefore, the holy one to be born will be called the Son of God. ³⁶ And consider your relative Elizabeth—even she has conceived a son

in her old age, and this is the sixth month for her who was called childless. [37] For nothing will be impossible with God."

[38] "See, I am the Lord's servant," said Mary. "May it happen to me as you have said." Then the angel left her.

Mary's Visit to Elizabeth

[39] In those days Mary set out and hurried to a town in the hill country of Judah [40] where she entered Zechariah's house and greeted Elizabeth. [41] When Elizabeth heard Mary's greeting, the baby leaped inside her, and Elizabeth was filled with the Holy Spirit. [42] Then she exclaimed with a loud cry, "Blessed are you among women, and your child will be blessed! [43] How could this happen to me, that the mother of my Lord should come to me? [44] For you see, when the sound of your greeting reached my ears, the baby leaped for joy inside me. [45] Blessed is she who has believed that the Lord would fulfill what he has spoken to her!"

Mary's Praise

[46] And Mary said:

> My soul magnifies the Lord,
> [47] and my spirit rejoices in God my Savior,
> [48] because he has looked with favor
> on the humble condition of his servant.
> Surely, from now on all generations
> will call me blessed,
> [49] because the Mighty One
> has done great things for me,
> and his name is holy.
> [50] His mercy is from generation to generation
> on those who fear him.
> [51] He has done a mighty deed with his arm;
> he has scattered the proud
> because of the thoughts of their hearts;
> [52] he has toppled the mighty from their thrones
> and exalted the lowly.
> [53] He has satisfied the hungry with good things
> and sent the rich away empty.
> [54] He has helped his servant Israel,
> remembering his mercy
> [55] to Abraham and his descendants forever,
> just as he spoke to our ancestors.

[56] And Mary stayed with her about three months; then she returned to her home.

Notes

JOHN

FROM CHAPTER 2

The First Sign: Turning Water into Wine

¹ On the third day a wedding took place in Cana of Galilee. Jesus's mother was there, ² and Jesus and his disciples were invited to the wedding as well. ³ When the wine ran out, Jesus's mother told him, "They don't have any wine."

⁴ "What has this concern of yours to do with me, woman?" Jesus asked. "My hour has not yet come."

⁵ "Do whatever he tells you," his mother told the servants.

⁶ Now six stone water jars had been set there for Jewish purification. Each contained twenty or thirty gallons.

⁷ "Fill the jars with water," Jesus told them. So they filled them to the brim. ⁸ Then he said to them, "Now draw some out and take it to the headwaiter." And they did.

⁹ When the headwaiter tasted the water (after it had become wine), he did not know where it came from—though the servants who had drawn the water knew. He called the groom ¹⁰ and told him, "Everyone sets out the fine wine first, then, after people are drunk, the inferior. But you have kept the fine wine until now."

¹¹ Jesus did this, the first of his signs, in Cana of Galilee. He revealed his glory, and his disciples believed in him.

¹² After this, he went down to Capernaum, together with his mother, his brothers, and his disciples, and they stayed there only a few days.

FROM CHAPTER 19

¹⁷ Carrying the cross by himself, he went out to what is called Place of the Skull, which in Aramaic is called *Golgotha*. ¹⁸ There they crucified him and two others with him, one on either side, with Jesus in the middle. ¹⁹ Pilate also had a sign made and put on the cross. It said: JESUS OF NAZARETH, THE KING OF THE JEWS. ²⁰ Many of the Jews read this sign, because the place where Jesus was crucified was near the city, and it was written in Aramaic, Latin, and Greek. ²¹ So the chief priests of the Jews said to Pilate, "Don't write, 'The king of the Jews,' but that he said, 'I am the king of the Jews.'"

²² Pilate replied, "What I have written, I have written."

²³ When the soldiers crucified Jesus, they took his clothes and divided them into four parts, a part for each soldier. They also took the tunic, which was seamless, woven in one piece from the top. ²⁴ So they said to one another, "Let's not tear it, but cast lots for it, to see who gets it." This happened that the Scripture might be fulfilled that says: They divided my clothes among themselves, and they cast lots for my clothing. This is what the soldiers did.

Jesus's Provision for His Mother

²⁵ Standing by the cross of Jesus were his mother, his mother's sister, Mary the wife of Clopas, and Mary Magdalene. ²⁶ When Jesus saw his mother and the disciple he loved standing there, he said to his mother, "Woman, here is your son." ²⁷ Then he said to the disciple, "Here is your mother." And from that hour the disciple took her into his home.

ACTS

FROM CHAPTER 1

United in Prayer

¹² Then they returned to Jerusalem from the Mount of Olives, which is near Jerusalem—a Sabbath day's journey away. ¹³ When they arrived, they went to the room upstairs where they were staying: Peter, John, James, Andrew, Philip, Thomas, Bartholomew, Matthew, James the son of Alphaeus, Simon the Zealot, and Judas the son of James. ¹⁴ They all were continually united in prayer, along with the women, including Mary the mother of Jesus, and his brothers.

01

What stood out to you or
surprised you about Mary's life?

02

From what you observed,
how would you describe Mary's
relationship with God?

03

What did you relate to in
Mary's story?

04

What connections did you see
in today's reading to the other
stories we've read?

COHEIRS IN CHRIST

The promises of inheritance, legacy, and place were never meant for Israel alone. Instead, through Israel, God planned to bring the nations to Himself. Through Jesus Christ, all believers—regardless of bloodline—are the children of Abraham by faith and belong to the family of God. We share in His inheritance as **coheirs** to the kingdom and the gifts of the Father.

MATTHEW

FROM CHAPTER 12

⁴⁶ While he was still speaking with the crowds, his mother and brothers were standing outside wanting to speak to him. ⁴⁷ Someone told him, "Look, your mother and your brothers are standing outside, wanting to speak to you."

⁴⁸ He replied to the one who was speaking to him, "Who is my mother and who are my brothers?" ⁴⁹ Stretching out his hand toward his disciples, he said, "Here are my mother and my brothers! ⁵⁰ For whoever does the will of my Father in heaven is my brother and sister and mother."

HEBREWS

FROM CHAPTER 2

Jesus and Humanity

⁵ For he has not subjected to angels the world to come that we are talking about. ⁶ But someone somewhere has testified:

What is man that you remember him,
or the son of man that you care for him?
⁷ You made him lower than the angels
for a short time;
you crowned him with glory and honor
⁸ and subjected everything under his feet.

For in subjecting everything to him, he left nothing that is not subject to him. As it is, we do not yet see everything subjected to him. ⁹ But we do see Jesus—made lower than the angels for a short time so that by God's grace he might taste death for everyone—crowned with glory and honor because he suffered death.

¹⁰ For in bringing many sons and daughters to glory, it was entirely appropriate that God—for whom and through whom all things exist—should make the pioneer of their salvation perfect through sufferings. ¹¹ For the one who

sanctifies and those who are sanctified all have one Father. That is why Jesus is not ashamed to call them brothers and sisters, [12] saying:

> I will proclaim your name to my brothers and sisters;
> I will sing hymns to you in the congregation.

[13] Again, I will trust in him. And again, Here I am with the children God gave me.

[14] Now since the children have flesh and blood in common, Jesus also shared in these,

so that through his death he might destroy the one holding the power of death—that is, the devil— [15] and free those who were held in slavery all their lives by the fear of death. [16] For it is clear that he does not reach out to help angels, but to help Abraham's offspring. [17] Therefore, he had to be like his brothers and sisters in every way, so that he could become a merciful and faithful high priest in matters pertaining to God, to make atonement for the sins of the people. [18] For since he himself has suffered when he was tempted, he is able to help those who are tempted.

ROMANS

FROM CHAPTER 4

The Promise Granted Through Faith

[13] For the promise to Abraham or to his descendants that he would inherit the world was not through the law, but through the righteousness that comes by faith. [14] If those who are of the law are heirs, faith is made empty and the promise nullified, [15] because the law produces wrath. And where there is no law, there is no transgression.

[16] This is why the promise is by faith, so that it may be according to grace, to guarantee it to all the descendants—not only to the one who is of the law but also to the one who is of Abraham's faith. He is the father of us all.

GALATIANS

FROM CHAPTER 3

Sons and Heirs

[27] For those of you who were baptized into Christ have been clothed with Christ. [28] There is no Jew or Greek, slave or free, male and female; since you are all one in Christ Jesus. [29] And if you belong to Christ, then you are Abraham's seed, heirs according to the promise.

Notes

WHAT IS THE SIGNIFICANCE OF "SONS"?

As mentioned on Day 1, the firstborn son was the one who typically inherited the father's wealth. When Paul reminds us that our inheritance in Christ is that of God's sons, it means we are welcomed and treated as coheirs with Christ, the firstborn Son, who receives what belongs to the Father. We all—male and female—have equal rights as His children to a full inheritance in Christ.

ROMANS

FROM CHAPTER 8

The Holy Spirit's Ministries

[12] So then, brothers and sisters, we are not obligated to the flesh to live according to the flesh, [13] because if you live according to the flesh, you are going to die. But if by the Spirit you put to death the deeds of the body, you will live. [14] For all those led by God's Spirit are God's sons. [15] For you did not receive a spirit of slavery to fall back into fear. Instead, you received the Spirit of adoption, by whom we cry out, "*Abba*, Father!" [16] The Spirit himself testifies together with our spirit that we are God's children, [17] and if children, also heirs—heirs of God and coheirs with Christ—if indeed we suffer with him so that we may also be glorified with him.

EPHESIANS

FROM CHAPTER 3

Paul's Ministry to the Gentiles

[1] For this reason, I, Paul, the prisoner of Christ Jesus on behalf of you Gentiles— [2] assuming you have heard about the administration of God's grace that he gave me for you. [3] The mystery was made known to me by revelation, as I have briefly written above. [4] By reading this you are able to understand my insight into the mystery of Christ. [5] This was not made known to people in other generations as it is now revealed to his holy apostles and prophets by the Spirit: [6] The Gentiles are coheirs, members of the same body, and partners in the promise in Christ Jesus through the gospel. [7] I was made a servant of this gospel by the gift of God's grace that was given to me by the working of his power.

[8] This grace was given to me—the least of all the saints—to proclaim to the Gentiles the incalculable riches of Christ, [9] and to shed light for all about the administration of the mystery hidden for ages in God who created all things. [10] This is so that God's multi-faceted wisdom may now be made known through the church to the rulers and authorities in the heavens. [11] This is according to his eternal purpose accomplished in Christ Jesus our Lord. [12] In him we have boldness and confident access through faith in him.

ROMANS

Death Through Adam and Life Through Christ

[12] Therefore, just as sin entered the world through one man, and death through sin, in this way death spread to all people, because all sinned. [13] In fact, sin was in the world before the law, but sin is not charged to a person's account when there is no law. [14] Nevertheless, death reigned from Adam to Moses, even over those who did not sin in the likeness of Adam's transgression. He is a type of the Coming One.

[15] But the gift is not like the trespass. For if by the one man's trespass the many died, how much more have the grace of God and the gift which comes through the grace of the one man Jesus Christ overflowed to the many. [16] And the gift is not like the one man's sin, because from one sin came the judgment, resulting in condemnation, but from many trespasses came the gift, resulting in justification. [17] If by the one man's trespass, death reigned through that one man, how much more will those who receive the overflow of grace and the gift of righteousness reign in life through the one man, Jesus Christ.

Notes

Response:

REFLECT

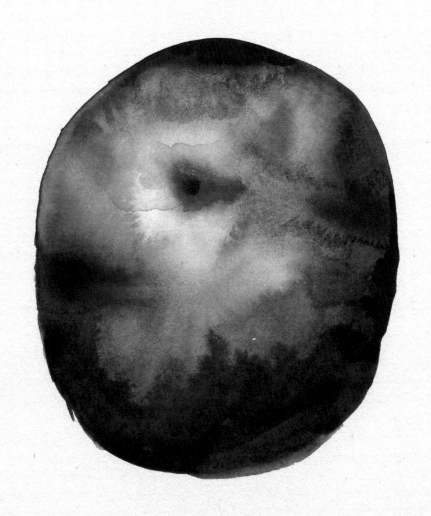

What does it mean to be part of God's spiritual family?

What does it mean to share in Jesus's inheritance?

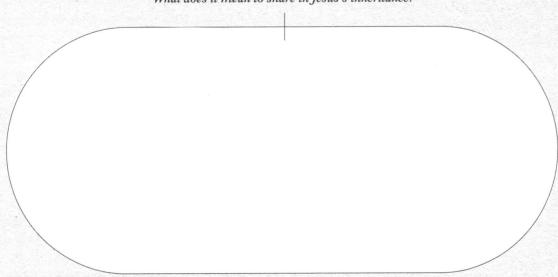

THINK BACK OVER THE LAST FIVE WEEKS OF READING
AS YOU ANSWER THESE FINAL QUESTIONS.

*Throughout this reading plan, how did you see God
keep His promise to make a people for Himself?*

How is Jesus the fulfillment of that promise?

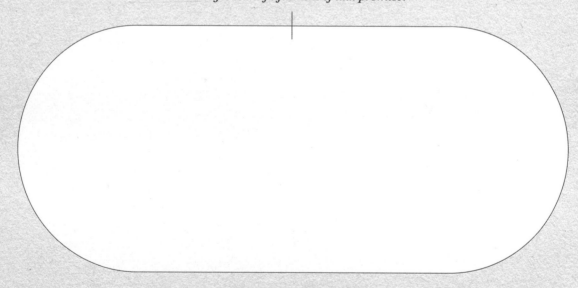

How does Jesus's own ancestry, and your place in the family of God, give you hope for the brokenness you experience in your earthly family?

How does it give you hope in your own still-unfolding part of the story?

GRACE DAY

Take this day to catch up on your reading, pray,
and rest in the presence of the Lord.

HE HAS HELPED HIS SERVANT ISRAEL,
REMEMBERING HIS MERCY TO ABRAHAM
AND HIS DESCENDANTS FOREVER.

LUKE 1:54–55

WEEKLY  TRUTH

Scripture is God-breathed and true. When we memorize it, we carry the good news of Jesus with us wherever we go.

For this study we have worked to memorize Romans 8:14–17. Spend some time reviewing the whole passage. As you do, celebrate the access believers have to God the Father through Christ, and the reality that He has adopted us as His children.

[14] FOR ALL THOSE LED BY GOD'S SPIRIT ARE GOD'S SONS. [15] FOR YOU DID NOT RECEIVE A SPIRIT OF SLAVERY TO FALL BACK INTO FEAR. INSTEAD, YOU RECEIVED THE SPIRIT OF ADOPTION, BY WHOM WE CRY OUT, "ABBA, FATHER!" [16] THE SPIRIT HIMSELF TESTIFIES TOGETHER WITH OUR SPIRIT THAT WE ARE GOD'S CHILDREN, [17] AND IF CHILDREN, ALSO HEIRS—HEIRS OF GOD AND COHEIRS WITH CHRIST—IF INDEED WE SUFFER WITH HIM SO THAT WE MAY ALSO BE GLORIFIED WITH HIM.

ROMANS 8:14–17

See tips for memorizing Scripture on page 172.

BUT TO ALL WHO DID RECEIVE HIM, HE
GAVE THEM THE RIGHT TO BE CHILDREN
OF GOD, TO THOSE WHO BELIEVE IN HIS
NAME, WHO WERE BORN, NOT OF NATURAL
DESCENT, OR OF THE WILL OF THE FLESH,
OR OF THE WILL OF MAN, BUT OF GOD.

JOHN 1:12–13

Tips for Memorizing Scripture

At She Reads Truth, we believe Scripture memorization is an important discipline in your walk with God. Committing God's Truth to memory means He can minister to us—and we can minister to others—through His Word no matter where we are. As you approach the Weekly Truth passage in this book, try these memorization tips to see which techniques work best for you!

STUDY IT

Study the passage in its biblical context and ask yourself a few questions before you begin to memorize it: What does this passage say? What does it mean? How would I say this in my own words? What does it teach me about God? Understanding what the passage means helps you know why it is important to carry it with you wherever you go.

Break the passage into smaller sections, memorizing a phrase at a time.

PRAY IT

Use the passage you are memorizing as a prompt for prayer.

WRITE IT

Dedicate a notebook to Scripture memorization and write the passage over and over again.

Diagram the passage after you write it out. Place a square around the verbs, underline the nouns, and circle any adjectives or adverbs. Say the passage aloud several times, emphasizing the verbs as you repeat it. Then do the same thing again with the nouns, then the adjectives and adverbs.

Write out the first letter of each word in the passage somewhere you can reference it throughout the week as you work on your memorization.

Use a whiteboard to write out the passage. Erase a few words at a time as you continue to repeat it aloud. Keep erasing parts of the passage until you have it all committed to memory.

CREATE

If you can, make up a tune for the passage to sing as you go about your day, or try singing it to the tune of a favorite song.

Sketch the passage, visualizing what each phrase would look like in the form of a picture. Or, try using calligraphy or altering the style of your handwriting as you write it out.

Use hand signals or signs to come up with associations for each word or phrase and repeat the movements as you practice.

SAY IT

Repeat the passage out loud to yourself as you are going through the rhythm of your day—getting ready, pouring your coffee, waiting in traffic, or making dinner.

Listen to the passage read aloud to you.

Record a voice memo on your phone and listen to it throughout the day or play it on an audio Bible.

SHARE IT

Memorize the passage with a friend, family member, or mentor. Spontaneously challenge each other to recite the passage, or pick a time to review your passage and practice saying it from memory together.

Send the passage as an encouraging text to a friend, testing yourself as you type to see how much you have memorized so far.

KEEP AT IT!

Set reminders on your phone to prompt you to practice your passage.

Purchase a She Reads Truth 12 Card Set or keep a stack of note cards with Scripture you are memorizing by your bed. Practice reciting what you've memorized previously before you go to sleep, ending with the passages you are currently learning. If you wake up in the middle of the night, review them again instead of grabbing your phone. Read them out loud before you get out of bed in the morning.

CSB BOOK ABBREVIATIONS

OLD TESTAMENT

GN Genesis	**JB** Job	**HAB** Habakkuk	**PHP** Philippians
EX Exodus	**PS** Psalms	**ZPH** Zephaniah	**COL** Colossians
LV Leviticus	**PR** Proverbs	**HG** Haggai	**1TH** 1 Thessalonians
NM Numbers	**EC** Ecclesiastes	**ZCH** Zechariah	**2TH** 2 Thessalonians
DT Deuteronomy	**SG** Song of Solomon	**MAL** Malachi	**1TM** 1 Timothy
JOS Joshua	**IS** Isaiah		**2TM** 2 Timothy
JDG Judges	**JR** Jeremiah		**TI** Titus
RU Ruth	**LM** Lamentations	**NEW TESTAMENT**	**PHM** Philemon
1SM 1 Samuel	**EZK** Ezekiel	**MT** Matthew	**HEB** Hebrews
2SM 2 Samuel	**DN** Daniel	**MK** Mark	**JMS** James
1KG 1 Kings	**HS** Hosea	**LK** Luke	**1PT** 1 Peter
2KG 2 Kings	**JL** Joel	**JN** John	**2PT** 2 Peter
1CH 1 Chronicles	**AM** Amos	**AC** Acts	**1JN** 1 John
2CH 2 Chronicles	**OB** Obadiah	**RM** Romans	**2JN** 2 John
EZR Ezra	**JNH** Jonah	**1CO** 1 Corinthians	**3JN** 3 John
NEH Nehemiah	**MC** Micah	**2CO** 2 Corinthians	**JD** Jude
EST Esther	**NAH** Nahum	**GL** Galatians	**RV** Revelation
		EPH Ephesians	

BIBLIOGRAPHY

Anderson, Kyle G. "Jesus, Genealogy of" in *The Lexham Bible Dictionary*, edited by John D. Barry et al. Bellingham: Lexham Press, 2016.

Blum, Edwin A., and Trevin Wax, eds. *CSB Study Bible: Notes*. Nashville: Holman Bible Publishers, 2017.

Book of Common Prayer and Administration of the Sacraments and other Rites and Ceremonies of the Church. New York: Church Publishing, Inc., 1789.

Branch, Robin Gallaher and Lee E. Klosinski. "Son," in *Eerdmans Dictionary of the Bible*, edited by David Noel Freedman, Allen C. Myers, and Astrid B. Beck. Grand Rapids: W.B. Eerdmans, 2000.

Senior, Donald. "Son of Man," in *Eerdmans Dictionary of the Bible*, edited by David Noel Freedman, Allen C. Myers, and Astrid B. Beck. Grand Rapids: W.B. Eerdmans, 2000.

Shields, Martin A. "Genealogy," in *The Lexham Bible Dictionary*, edited by John D. Barry et al. Bellingham: Lexham Press, 2016.

Wohlleben, Peter. *The Hidden Life of Trees: What They Feel, How They Communicate*. New York: HarperCollins, 2017.

JOIN THE
CONVERSATION

Download the **She Reads Truth app** to connect with other Shes who are reading God's Word right along with you. Hop into the community discussion for engagement around your daily Scripture reading, moments of reflection, and more!

You just spent 35 days in the Word of God!

MY FAVORITE DAY OF
THIS READING PLAN:

ONE THING I LEARNED
ABOUT GOD:

WHAT WAS GOD DOING IN
MY LIFE DURING THIS STUDY?

HOW DID I FIND DELIGHT IN GOD'S WORD?

WHAT DID I LEARN THAT I WANT TO SHARE
WITH SOMEONE ELSE?

A SPECIFIC SCRIPTURE THAT
ENCOURAGED ME:

A SPECIFIC SCRIPTURE THAT
CHALLENGED AND CONVICTED ME: